W9-BOG-630

THE
COMPLETE
GUIDE TO **Black
& White**
Digital Photography

# THE
# COMPLETE
# GUIDE TO
# Black
# & White
## Digital Photography

## MICHAEL FREEMAN

## LARK BOOKS

A Division of Sterling Publishing Co., Inc.
New York / London

The Complete Guide to Black & White Digital Photography

**Library of Congress Cataloging-in-Publication Data**

Freeman, Michael, 1945-
  The complete guide to black & white digital photography / Michael H. Freeman.
-- 1st
ed.
       p. cm.

  Includes bibliographical references and index.
  1.  Photography--Digital techniques. 2.  Black-and-white photography  I.
Title.
  TR267.F7385 2009
  778.3--dc22
                                    2009015555
10 9 8 7 6 5 4 3 2 1

First Edition
Published by Lark Books, A Division of
Sterling Publishing Co., Inc.
387 Park Avenue South, New York, N.Y. 10016

Text © The Ilex Press Limited 2010
Images © Michael Freeman except where noted otherwise

This book was conceived, designed, and produced by:
ILEX
210 High Street
Lewes
BN7 2NS
United Kingdom

Distributed in Canada by Sterling Publishing,
c/o Canadian Manda Group, 165 Dufferin Street

Toronto, Ontario, Canada M6K 3H6

The written instructions, photographs, designs, patterns, and projects in this
volume are intended for the personal use of the reader and may be reproduced for
that purpose only. Any other use, especially commercial use, is forbidden under law
without written permission of the publisher. The works represented are the original
creations of the contributing artists. All artists retain copyrights on their individual
works, except as noted.

Every effort has been made to ensure that all the information in this book is
accurate. However, due to differing conditions, tools, and individual skills, the
publisher cannot be responsible for any injuries, losses, and other damages that may
result from the use of the information in this book. Because specifications may be
changed by the manufacturer without notice, the contents of this book may not
necessarily agree with software and equipment changes made after publication.

If you have questions or comments about this book, please contact:
Lark Books
67 Broadway
Asheville, NC 28801
(828) 253-0467

Manufactured in China

All rights reserved

ISBN 13: 978-1-60059-523-3

To download illustrations for Photoshop exercises, Please visit:
**http://www.web-linked.com/cgbwus/**

For information about custom editions, special sales, premium and corporate
purchases, please contact Sterling Special Sales Department at 800-805-5489 or
specialsales@sterlingpub.com.

# CONTENTS

# SECTION 3
# CREATIVE CHOICES 138

# SECTION 4
# PRINTING & DISPLAY 188

# INTRODUCTION

**B**lack-and-white photography occupies a unique place in the world of art and imaging, all the more surprising because within the world of photography it is taken so much for granted. What I will attempt in this book is to jolt black and white out of its normally complacent position, and in this I'm helped by the completely changed circumstances of digital photography.

Why complacent? Because black and white has become so established as the senior tradition of photography over the course of more than a century that its reasons for being are only rarely questioned. For many people, perhaps most, black-and-white photography just "is." I just re-read a volume on the history of photography by Ian Jeffrey, titled *Photography: A Concise History* that appeared in Thames & Hudson's World of Art series, where black and white is so much assumed to be center stage that color fills just three pages out of 240. This is by no means unusual, but it is hard to justify simply on the grounds that there were more years spent in black and white than in color. It also won't do for the modern world of digital photography, in which the choice of one or the other is in the face of every photographer each time he or she decides to process on the computer.

It seems that most photographers, when they are shooting or processing, inhabit a world of photography alone, and only a few see their work in the wider context of art. I have to say "seems" because there is no way of quantifying this, but what is not in doubt is this: in the entire body of writing and discussion on photography, references to painting or any other graphic art are very thin on the ground. This is a little strange, not to say short-sighted, but it's part of the reality of our photographic world. There are historical reasons for this, as there are, well, philosophical reasons.

From the other side of the fence—the unconstrained art side—there has been more acceptance of photography. A fairly recent phenomenon, which tends to set many photographers' teeth on edge, is the appropriation of photography by artists who do not claim to be primarily photographers. In other words, contemporary artists invade photography more than photography invades art.

And it is this unmistakable sense of photography being its own world, very largely self-contained, that allows us to be complacent about black and white. It's just something that photography grew up with. Now, however, things are on the move, which is what I want to explore in this book.

# THE BLACK & WHITE TRADITION

Digital photography has very clearly changed the way we can shoot in black and white, and it is perfectly obvious that by far the most important practical difference between a sensor and film is that now you can have both color and monochrome from the same shot. There is no prior choice to be made, no decision to load black-and-white film rather than color film before setting out.

As a result, most of what is written and discussed about digital black and white focuses on the practicalities—how to convert, how to adjust channels in order to alter the brightness of different colors as they appear in grayscale, how to achieve the "look" and grain of a favored black-and-white emulsion, and so on. All essential and all valuable topics to study, but all skipping the one key issue: More fundamental than the "how" of shooting monochrome is why and when. There's nothing too complicated about explaining how to achieve all the various kinds of monochrome effect from a digital image—and I hasten to add that this is all included in this book—but much more interesting is the choice to make the image in black-and-white rather than in the more obvious color.

This choice transcends the difference between sensors and film, and it draws us into the long and rich tradition of black-and-white photography. Film and earlier processes of course weigh heavily on this tradition, and for this reason I make no apology for looking at the past. Black-and-white film photography, its image qualities and processes, have a great deal to teach us. Not only this, but black-and-white photography is traditionally more strongly associated with art than is color, and there are lessons to learn also from monochrome painting. The common theme running through all of this is restricting the palette. What sets black and white apart from color is that it is not the way we see the world and it does not pretend to represent reality. It is a translation of a view into a special medium with very particular characteristics. As we will see, there has been a changing perception of black and white as a medium in photography. Crudely put, it began as necessity, then became accepted as normal, and now, with the full choice of color (and any kind of color) coupled with the infinite processing possibilities of digital images, it is a creative choice.

# MONOCHROME IN FINE ART

**Monochrome—black and white even more—occupies the same minority position in the history of art as color did in photography's first hundred years.**

The reasons for this complete reversal of status bear some examination, because they help us to understand the independent way in which photography has developed. Independent of the rest of art, that is. Monochrome in photography is used more or less interchangeably with black and white, but not quite so in the wider world of art. Monochrome painting is largely a twentieth century phenomenon, whereas the history of black and white is mainly that of ink, one of the most ancient of media.

The most common source of ink has always been carbon, held together by binding agents, and in the earliest times it can have been only a short step from touching the lamp black or soot over a fire to painting and drawing. The use of black ink in art was universal, because of this ease of production. Ink appears in China at least 5,000 years ago and in India at least 6,000 years ago. Other sources were ferrous sulfate, tannins from gallnuts, cuttlefish, and hawthorne bark, among others.

Its main uses in Western art have been for drawing and for indirect application such as etching and woodcuts. In East Asia, directly applied by brush in the form of calligraphy and scroll paintings, it enjoyed a higher status. There, laid down in broad strokes with brushes, its qualities in covering an area of paper were more critically acknowledged. The immediate commitment needed with brush strokes proved to be a fertile ground for developing great skill, and for a finely tuned aesthetic appreciation.

Monochrome painting in the West, known as "grisailles" (from the French gris, meaning gray), is known from the Renaissance onwards, but occasionally rather than often, and a typical use was in frescoes in shades of gray and/or brown. Its use was often dictated by a need to execute quickly and cheaply more than for aesthetic reasons. It was the rise of abstract art in the twentieth century that led to more experimentation with painting in a single color, and this color was not confined to black or white. The Suprematist painter Kasimir Malevich produced black on white, and white on white paintings from 1913, Ben Nicholson produced all-white low reliefs in the 1930s, Yves Klein created a series of paintings in blue in the 1950s, Agnes Martin in black, white, and brown in the 1960s, Mark Rothko's late paintings from the 1960s, also the contemporary Chuck Close in black and white, and the Chinese contemporary artist Shao Fan in black on black, among others.

The connection between monochrome painting and monochrome photography is notably absent from discussions of art history, but it seems to me a fruitful area, especially now that digital capture makes it a free choice for photographers. The reasons why painters choose to work with a severely restricted palette may not be very different from the preferences of photographers in black and white. In the twentieth-century West, monochrome was frequently tied to simplicity of form, particularly in a geometric sense. The short-lived Russian Suprematist movement (not at all to be confused with Supremacism) set the scene for this, with Kasemir Malevich's squares and circles in black and in white, and it can be seen later in Ben Nicholson's white works and in Agnes Martin's hand-drawn grids. Some hint of the emotional significance of monochrome comes through in Malevich's writing when describing his Black Square, 1913: "I felt only night within me and it was then that I conceived the new art, which I called Suprematism." This emotion-through-monochrome is a recurring theme in photography, as can be seen in the enduring work of, among others, Don McCullin, Bill Brandt, and Harry Callahan.

The American painter Agnes Martin moved in the early 1960s from early experiments with bands of bright color to a severely muted palette, coinciding with a trend in American art at the time towards reductivism—using a few elements only, in color, tone, and form, to avoid representation and illusion. She dated her attaining artistic maturity to this time, saying. "I finally got to an absolute abstract painting."

Significantly, Martin was interested in Chinese art, art philosophy, and Taoism, and from this in the importance of communicating absence. One of her statements reads, "Two late Tang dishes, one with a flower image, one empty. The empty form goes all the way to heaven." The monochrome feature of Martin's work is just one of the methods she employed to simplify in order to make a spiritual connection, as the statement alludes to. She defined art as "the concrete representation of our most subtle feelings," and subtlety of color and tone were very evidently a key method in this exploration.

Better known, Abstract Expressionist Mark Rothko also moved through his painting career from

**Agnes Martin**
*One of Agnes Martin's geometrical series, in which she explores "subtle feelings" in a manner influenced by Chinese art.*

# MONOCHROME IN FINE ART

colorful towards a restricted palette, and his last paintings were in near-black and near-gray. His Black-Form paintings in particular, never shown together during his lifetime, appear at first glance a solid black, but reveal a slow build-up of layering and very fine gradation. This has the effect of drawing the viewer into a separate world with its own range of luminosity. As with some of the low-key photography we will see later in the book, once the viewer accepts the very different range of tone from the surrounding world, the perception of fine shading and minute tonal differences is heightened.

A contemporary Chinese artist following this route is Shao Fan. His work, like that of the literati in earlier centuries, is broad-ranging, from sculpture to calligraphy to architecture, garden design, and painting—a very Chinese approach to the arts. In his black series, dating from 1998, Shao Fan works in oil on canvas in a tonal range that rarely rises above dark gray. He writes, "The low key and very weak contrast create an atmosphere of the supernatural. It renews our attention to the insignificant, and to things in the process of disappearing, a simultaneous feeling of distance and attraction." Subtle differences in color, akin to what traditional black-and-white photographers think of as toning, play an important part.

Another contemporary artist, whose work conflates painting and sculpture and who is drawn to the subtle

**Chinese calligraphy**
*A contemporary Chinese artist who works principally in brush and ink. The modulations of a single color—black—through skillful handling of the heavily loaded brush initiated a strong Asian tradition of black and white.*

**Japanese calligraphy**
*A modern calligraphic figure, by Japanese artist Takeshi Nagasaki, created in ink with a white paint overlay. The fading tail of a stroke is of great importance.*

**Alternative light**
*A number of different treatments of black subjects indicate the potential range of even a narrow palette when interpreted through exposure choices.*

# MONOCHROME IN FINE ART

and low-chromaticity end of the scale, is London-based Yukako Shibata. Monochrome for her means working within one specific hue, often modulating it by means of reflection from close external surfaces, such as a white wall. She explores low chromaticity in her work and a major inspiration is what Shibata calls "the fugitive colors of nature." Delicacy, very fine transitions of hue, and a sense of calm rather than stridency mark her interests. Painters, of course, can choose to see and interpret with complete freedom, but now digital processing gives photographers the same opportunities, and restricting the color range definitely encourages a contemplative approach to imagery.

As we will see time and again in photography, restricting the palette allows the artist to concentrate fully on the subtleties of tone. As any calligrapher knows, the quality of black is infinitely variable, and goes far beyond any simple numerical measurement of darkness. The ways in which black varies as the brush is lifted slightly on the paper during a stroke find their equivalent in delicate tonal adjustments during the processing of a black-and-white photograph.

**White art**
Imprint, *a white-on-white piece by Yukako Shibata, in which a high key is explored. The physical indentations are given an illusory quality by having shadows painted into them.*

THE BLACK & WHITE TRADITION

**Monochrome**
*As in photography, monochrome can mean a color other than black. In this piece by Yukako Shibata, a specific blue casts a reflection on the white surface, yet is unseen as it is painted on the inside of the frame.*

# THE PHOTOGRAPHIC TRADITION

**The technical history of photography actually forced monochrome on us in the most obvious way. Quite simply, light-sensitive materials that could be used to capture an image on a flat surface reacted to light in total, undivided by wavelength.**

Recording the color of a scene meant filtering the light through a set of at least three colored transparent filters, and that involved a much more complicated feat of technology than simple monochrome.

Even so, it might come as a surprise to many people to learn that the first permanent color photograph, taken by James Clark Maxwell, was as early as 1861. Various processes were invented between then and the 1930s, but technical limitations prevented their mass use, and it was not until the Eastman Kodak Company introduced the integral tri-pack color film in 1935 that black and white had any realistic competition as a medium. This was the classic Kodachrome.

The earliest photograph, taken by Niepce in 1826, used a substance that hardened rather than darkened when exposed to light, a type of asphalt that was already used in engraving. Coated on a pewter plate, the asphalt was exposed in a camera to a view from Niepce's window. After about eight hours, the asphalt exposed to the bright parts of the scene was so hardened that it resisted the solvent, which Niepce then poured over it; the unexposed, dark parts washed away.

Within twelve years, Niepce's partner, Daguerre, had discovered a more sensitive photographic plate. Copper, already coated with silver, was sensitized by exposure to iodine vapor rising from heated iodine crystals. After the picture had been taken, the image, not yet visible, was developed by mercury vapor—a dangerous process with health hazards not fully appreciated at the time. The image was finally fixed with hyposulphite of soda, and the result was a finely detailed, delicate photograph. However, because of its mirror-like finish, it had to be viewed at a particular angle and, being a positive, could not be used to make a quantity of prints. Nevertheless, the exposure time had been reduced from eight hours to between twenty and thirty minutes, and although this was still too long for portraiture, which had to wait for later improvements, photography had finally become a practical possibility.

The daguerreotype was soon challenged by an alternative process, the calotype, which used paper instead of a metal plate and was closer to modern films in that it produced a negative image that could be used to make as many positive prints as the photographer wanted. The reproductive capacity made this process

**Daguerrotype**
*A simple daguerrotype camera in wood, with a focusing mechanism in which the rear plate-holder is racked out backwards. Accompanying it, a daguerrotype portrait of Cyrus West Field, the American who laid the first transatlantic telegraph cable.*

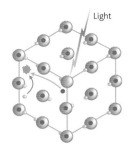

Silver Ion
Bromide Ion

nsitivity
Speck

Free
ilver Ion

Light

1. Floating ions

2. Ions attracted

3. Photon strike

4. After exposure

an important rival to the daguerreotype, despite the poorer quality of the image. The inventor was the Englishman William Henry Fox Talbot (1800-1877) who, starting with a high quality writing paper, added coatings of silver nitrate and potassium iodide, followed by a solution of gallic acid and silver nitrate to sensitize the paper. Having made the exposure, the paper was developed in a second application of the gallic acid/silver nitrate solution. Once dry, the paper negative was ready for making contact prints.

The next important step in the progress of emulsion was the invention in 1851 of the collodion process by Frederick Scott Archer (1813-1857). Also known as the wet-plate process, the collodion process quickly replaced other systems because, despite the great inconvenience of preparing the plates, which had to be carried out on the spot just before taking the picture, it allowed exposures of as little as ten seconds. To achieve this great sensitivity, the photographer had to pour collodion, a solution containing potassium iodide, onto a glass plate, tilt it in different directions

**Collodion**
*A collodion wet-plate kit from the nineteenth century. The entire process, from coating through exposure to processing, had to be complete before the plate dried.*

until the coating was even, and then quickly dip the plate in a silver nitrate solution. Because the sensitivity was largely lost when the collodion dried, the plate had to be exposed wet, making life very difficult for the photographer on location.

By the 1870s, an emulsion made up of gelatin and silver bromide had been invented as a dry substitute for collodion, and soon plates were being mass-produced. Although glass (which is bulky and easily broken) has now been replaced by flexible film, black-and-white emulsion remains basically the same: the light-sensitive crystals, known as grains, are embedded in a layer of gelatin. Film was originally made of celluloid, but has since moved through nitro-cellulose to cellulose acetate to the immensely stable synthetic polymers of today. Whatever its composition, the use of film made it possible to roll up long strips of emulsion, the basis of motion picture film, 35mm film, and rollfilm.

The precise sequence of events that follows the exposure of film to light is complex. First, light releases photoelectrons, and these combine with silver ions to produce silver atoms, which form around small specks of impurity scattered throughout each silver halide crystal. At this stage, there is still no visible image on the film, and it takes a chemical developer to produce it. Development blackens the parts of the emulsion that were exposed to light, by reducing the grains of silver halide to metallic silver, which is dark. Each grain is either developed—that is, blackened—or not; there are no halfway stages of gray. The final result, with a range of tones in the negative, is due to the number of developed grains in any small part of the film: if only a few have been developed, scattered among many undeveloped ones, the tone will be a light gray, but if all have reacted, then the film will be black.

### 1. Floating ions
*In a schematic version of one grain of silver bromide, pairs of silver and bromide ions are held together by an electrical charge. The silver ions lack one electron, and so have a positive charge. The bromide ions have an extra electron, and are negatively charged. Specks of silfer sulphide and occasional free ions complete the structure.*

### 2. Ions attracted
*When a photon of light strikes the crystal, it gives extra energy to the electron of a bromide ion, allowing it to move around the crystal. The bromide ion then attracts and bonds to a positively charged free silver ion. Specks of impurity, such as silver sulphide, tend to attract this new bonding and so are known as sensitivity specks.*

### 3. Photon strike
*As more photons of light strike the crystal, more electrons are released. These and more silver ions migrate to the sensitivity speck like the others. The combination of ions and electrons creates silver metal, although this is invisible at this point.*

### 4. After exposure
*After the full exposure to light, the chemical change has occurred but needs the action of a developing fluid to magnify it several million times so that it becomes visible to the eye.*

# THE PHOTOGRAPHIC TRADITION

**Landscapes**
*The Cuillins, Isle of Skye, Scotland. Landscape was the first subject of photography, and persists.*

# THE PHOTOGRAPHIC TRADITION

## WHITE SKY VS TONEMAPPED

A modern photograph, but processed in two ways: as blue-sensitive, demonstrating the sensitivity of early emulsions, and as a tonemapped HDR image, from five exposures, to reveal all tones from the original scene.

**Silhouette and flare**
*LEFT The limited response of film and sensors to the full dynamic range of sunlit scenes has become accepted as a photographic characteristic—objects in silhouette, and glittering flare from highlights, for example.*

**Crater Lake
Edward Curtis**
*RIGHT Early emulsions, such as those used by Edward Curtis, who photographed the American West, were sensitive to blue and not to red, which resulted in a look that was accepted at the time—white skies, dark skin—and which Curtis used compositionally.* Courtsesy Corbis.

# WAVELENGTH & SENSITIVITY

**T**his may sound too obvious to mention, and most camera sensors and lenses achieve results so perfectly acceptable that we rarely question it, but things become interesting in this area when you shoot for monochrome. At heart, this is a technical issue involving wavelength.

Our eyes are sensitive to a very small part of the electromagnetic spectrum, from around 400 nm to 700 nm—what is called, obviously, the visible spectrum. In reasonably good light, the eye can distinguish millions of colors. It manages this because the cones are divided into three types: those sensitive to red, others to green, and others to blue. These three together embrace more or less the full spectrum, so that by varying the input from each, any other color can be made. In the case of our vision, this occurs in the brain, but the three kinds of receptor are not equally efficient. The eye is most sensitive to yellow-green, and least sensitive to blue; what we cannot see is ultra-violet, the reason being that the eye has two yellow filters, over the lens and over the fovea, which probably evolved to reduce chromatic aberration, at its greatest in violet and ultra-violet light.

Camera sensors do not match the eye's color response, and need both physical filters and special image processing to come close. Sensors, indeed, record monochrome, and the means for capturing color in the vast majority is a filter in front, simple in theory, called a Bayer array. This is a mosaic of red, green, and blue, each square of color sited over on photosite on the sensor. To correspond more closely with the human eye's extra sensitivity to green light, there are twice as many green filters in a Bayer array than there are red or blue. The human eye's peak sensitivity is in yellow-green at 555 nanometers; it reacts very poorly, by contrast, to wavelengths shorter than violet and longer than red. Sensors also differ from the Human Vision System in that they are sensitive to infrared, and so for normal cameras have added to them an infrared-cut filter (as we'll see on page 82, removing this is the way to customize a camera for infrared photography).

In our experience of colors, some hues are brighter than others: an average yellow, for example, is brighter to us than an average blue. If the tones in which different colors are reproduced in a black-and-white photograph approximate to this experience, the image seems realistic. The blue sensitivity of black-and-white film can result in clear skies that look too pale, but a yellow filter—which absorbs blue—restores the expected appearance.

The principle of this is straightforward. A colored filter placed in front of the lens will pass more of its own color and block the light of other colors. The contrast between, for example, a red tomato and green lettuce leaves in a salad is immediately obvious when viewed in color, but not at all in black and white.

**In normal color photography, one of the basic aims is to record the scene as it looks to the eye.**

**Eye's spectral sensitivity**
*The spectral sensitivity of the human eye is a combination of three kinds of cones, each sensitive to a section of wavelengths, and rods. It peaks in the yellow-green.*

THE BLACK & WHITE TRADITION

beta cones

gamma cones

rho cones

rods

All rods and cones

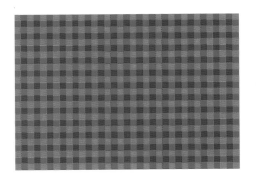

**Bayer filter pattern**
*A Bayer array, bonded to the front of a camera sensor, with one square covering one photosite.*

**Original**

**Desaturated**
*A straight desaturation of this image in a temple in Shanghai shows that the blue and orange are equal in brightness, yet the color perception imagines the warmer tone to be brighter.*

**Original**

**Desaturated**
*Straight desaturation, equal for all channels.*

**BLACK AND WHITE**

| | |
|---|---|
| REDS | -22% |
| YELLOWS | 181% |
| GREENS | 190% |
| CYANS | 60% |
| BLUES | 20% |
| MAGENTAS | 80% |

**BLACK AND WHITE**

| | |
|---|---|
| REDS | 211% |
| YELLOWS | 47% |
| GREENS | 40% |
| CYANS | 60% |
| BLUES | 20% |
| MAGENTAS | 80% |

**High Red**
*High red and lower greens creates high contrast with a light roof and dark surroundings.*

**BLACK AND WHITE**

| | |
|---|---|
| REDS | 122% |
| YELLOWS | 51% |
| GREENS | 47% |
| CYANS | 60% |
| BLUES | 20% |
| MAGENTAS | 80% |

**Light Red**
*A more naturalistic result keeps the red roof light (on the principle that warm colors are thought of as lighter), and the grass medium-dark.*

**Low Red**
*Lowering red and raising green is still high contrast, but opposite to "High Red."*

# BLACK & WHITE
# AS NORMALITY

**A black-and-white photograph is clearly some distance from actually representing a scene.**

ntil color film became practical and widely available, the very lack of color information was a definite drawback for many photographers and for publications that used photographs. And yet by about the 1930s, in documentary photography, led by news, black and white had become thoroughly accepted as a normal representation of events and the world in general. From the perspective of now, with color photography long established as the default, this may not be easy to appreciate fully, but in, say, Life magazine's and Picture Post's coverage of the Second World War, the veracity of monochrome was unquestioned, and the reading public managed without thinking to bridge the gap between the colored real world and the completely unsaturated image. Black-and-white imagery remained "normal" in newsprint until offset color became practical for dailies around the 1980s. How and why this happened is worth considering, because the decades of black-and-white "normality" impressed the monochrome image with a particular strength and legitimacy.

The onset of acceptance was slow and uneven, and can be argued to have been a special feature of documentary photography, where the aim was to show things "as they are," even though this is a loose concept open to various interpretations. Naturally, documentary photographers, always more concerned with the events in front of them than a creative or deliberate treatment of them, worked with whatever was available to them.

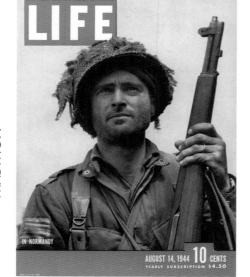

**Life magazine covers**
*For many years Life magazine presented a striking combination of a red masthead set against a strong black-and-white picture depicting current events. During the 50s color became more usual.*

Speed was a never-ending concern—the ability to capture movement in as many lighting conditions as possible. Even with fast lenses, documentary photography has relied on fast—more sensitive—recording media. This alone kept color at bay, as it was always easier to manufacture faster black-and-white emulsions than color emulsions. Kodak's Tri-X, with its nominal speed of 400 ISO, and its ability to be "pushed" in development considerably higher, became the most popular and widely used of all reportage films.

The period from the 1930s through the 1940s saw substantial technical progress in photography, from cameras to lenses to film. 35mm film, already used in cinematography, became the medium of choice after Oscar Barnack invented the Leica to use it. Loading, winding on, and unloading were faster, and as a result of this and other developments, reportage photography became ever more flexible and adaptable to changing situations. At the same time, this was socially and economically a disastrous period for much of the world, and photography concentrated on these more than ever before. Ian Jeffrey, writing in *Photography: A Concise History* (part of the Thames & Hudson *World of Art* series), took the view that "...during the 1930s photography's tasks were mainly social and reformist, for which urgent black-and-white was an apt medium." This is an exaggeratedly narrow view of 1930s photography en masse, and for its own convenience ignores a large area of news journalism, but the point is valid within its frame of reference. Sally Eauclaire, setting the scene for a discussion of how color photography became critically acceptable in the 1970s, wrote in *The New Color Photography*, "Black-and-white photography figures so predominantly in the documentary tradition that we might be conditioned to expect the news in tones, not chromes."

The legacy of this period, approximately from the 1930s through the early 1960s, is that even today black and white is accorded a respect for its documentary "correctness." So much so that in 1997,

Graham Clarke, writing in *The Photograph*, part of the *Oxford History of Art* series, could say, "The traditional canon of photography largely eschews color, so that we are faced with the paradox of photography's 'realism' being communicated in black and white… The most obvious aspect of this remains the traditional 'documentary' image, where the presence of color actually lessens the sense of the photograph's veracity as an image and witness. We equate black-and-white photographs with 'realism' and the authentic." Contemporary documentary photographers who stick to black and white as much as possible include Sebastiao Salgado, Chien-Chi Chang, and Richard Kalvar, among many others. Some photographers are certainly influenced in this by their preference for the medium of film, but Salgado, for example, has recently moved to digital after extensive testing, and is delighted with it. The medium for him is monochrome rather than film.

Other forms of photography encouraged different strategies. In the studio, for example, the best photographers quickly sidestepped the issue of lack of color and exploited black and white's essential qualities, lighting, and composing for drama, geometry, texture, or sensuousness, according to skill and taste.

From as early as the beginning of the 1930s, Horst P. Horst's Hollywood portraits and fashion shots, for example, are masterpieces of constructed lighting from which color would only have distracted. Portrait photography outside the studio could also make full use of black and white's strengths. Bill Brandt's bold use of dark and light masses, as in his portrait of playwright Harold Pinter on page 156, was another, more spontaneous approach.

And of course, with a full knowledge of the physics of light and the chemistry of reproduction, it was possible for a thoughtful photographer to justify the superiority of monochrome on philosophical grounds. Henri Cartier-Bresson wrote, "Color in photography is founded on a basic prism; for the time being, it cannot be otherwise, because we do not yet have the chemical processes that permit the complex breaking down and reconstitution of color (in the pastel range, for example, the gamut of greens is made up of 375 nuances!)." He went on to argue from this that, "For me, color is a very important medium of information, but it is very limited on the

**The Ermanox**
*Introduced in 1924, the year before the first Leica, the Emanox marked a step in making possible candid reportage photography. Even though it used glass plates, which were slow to change, its Ernostar f/1.8 lens was exceptionally fast.*

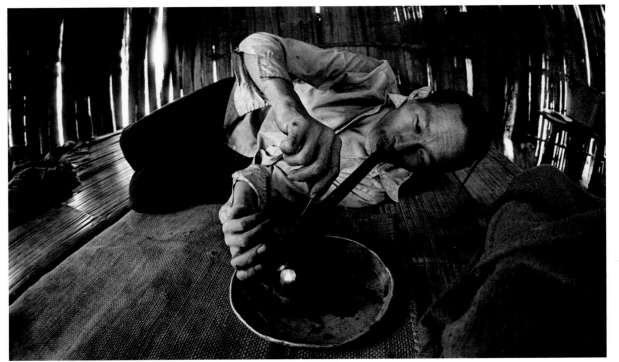

**Fast film**
*35mm camera and ISO 400 Tri-X film came to embody reportage photography— rapid shooting in available light of people and social issues—here an opium addict in northern Thailand.*

# BLACK & WHITE AS NORMALITY

reproduction-surface, which remains chemical and not transcendental, not intuitive, as it is in painting. As opposed to black, which has the most complex range, color, on the contrary, offers only a fragmentary range."

Paul Strand made a similar point in his objections to color: "It's a dye. It has no body or texture or density, as paint does." He continued, "So far, it doesn't do anything but add an uncomfortable element to a medium that's hard enough to control anyway," and this probably exposes his real concern. One of black-and-white photography's great joys and strengths is that it offers a different world from the one we experience, with less going on in it and therefore more to explore in the image qualities that it does offer. As in most human activity, the simpler the situation, the more effort can be put into what remains. In photography, then, restrict the medium and you increase the potential refinement, meaning that if you are faced with a scale of gray as opposed to a scale of color plus gray shades, as in the illustrations here, you pay much more attention to the subtleties of the gray scale. Strand, by the way, continued to refer to color photography as black and white that had been dyed.

Deeper than this was an understandable streak of conservatism that ran through many of the established photographers in the 1960s, the time that color was becoming a major force in photography. This conservatism was created because they had spent a lifetime, or part of it, mastering a medium that involved conceptualizing in black and white. It was not that there was much evidence or fear of losing the game, but rather that their black-and-white photography was more intellectual, crafted, dependent on a hard-won sensibility to how a raw scene from the world could be turned into a very different and specific art form. There was a distinct feeling at the higher end of photography until well into the 1980s that basically anyone could take a color image, because it simply reproduced what was there, but to make the shift to a unique medium was, simply, a higher calling. Hence the often pompous statements that were frequently

**The Mainbocher Corset**
*OPPOSITE PAGE*
*Horst P. Horst, 1939*
*One of the iconic photos
of the the twentith century.
(Courtesy the Art +
Commerce agency).*

**Bayon terrace**
*The upper terrace of the
Bayon in Angkor. The colors
in the scene are relatively
insignificant, and shooting in
black and white enables full
attention to be paid to the
modeling and the massing
of shadows and highlights.*

made. Walker Evans made the not-very-clever adaptation of Lord Acton's "Power tends to corrupt…" as "Color tends to corrupt photography and absolute color corrupts absolutely… There are four simple words for the matter which must be whispered: color photography is vulgar."

There is a definite sense in reading all these opinions from the 1970s and earlier of a rearguard action being fought to preserve black and white. It was clear to anyone who thought about it that photography was becoming simpler, available to all, and color photography was going to have its way in the mass market because it was simply what most people wanted. In the end, they need not have bothered so much. Yes, color did take over the world of photography, and even, from the 1980s onward, achieved artistic respectability at photography's more refined end. But far from spelling the demise of black

and white, it created a reason among many serious photographers for wanting a different medium, more refined, and definitely apart from the mass of snapshooters.

The argument hinges on color offering too much. The more that you can expect to capture in an image, the more difficult it is to put your personal stamp on the image and say "this is the way I see it, not the way it is." This was, and is, a genuine concern. A wider choice of materials, more and better tools, are a mixed blessing for any photographer or artist. On the one hand they make it possible to do new things and explore kinds of imagery that no-one tried until now. At the same time, however, they can offer too much choice, and distract. It usually helps to have a clear view when you create an image, and cluttering this up with more and more possibilities can just be a damaging nuisance. Cartier-Bresson, one of whose greatest skills

# BLACK & WHITE
# AS NORMALITY

was organizing the chaos of fleeting street scenes into compositional unity, said simply, "Imagine having to think about color on top of all this." It's easy to draw parallels with other camera-or-medium inventions. Zoom lenses, now standard, were not thought of as a universal blessing when they began to appear in the late 1950s. Quite apart from optical quality in the early zoom designs (a top-quality prime, that is fixed focal length, lens still sets the highest standard), they gave a new dimension to composition. Framing could be fine-tuned infinitely; great if you were a sports or event photographer shooting from a fixed position, but for many photographers it gives just an extra layer of choice, meaning more to think about, which can at times delay the shot by just enough to lose it.

And it goes much further than "how can we cope with all of this sensory input." Art can be many things,

but it is never about reproducing reality as perfectly as possible. There is always a translation of one kind or another—filtering the real through a creative imagination, if you like. It's tempting to argue that the new digital and totally flexible ways in which color can be handled, manipulated, corrected, and adjusted have actually furthered the cause of black and white. The division between monochrome and color has certainly disappeared with the easy ability to choose exactly how saturated or unsaturated any hue should be in an image. In that sense, black and white simply represents one end of a continuum, not on its own island. Later, in chapter 4, we'll be treating these shades of tone from the point of view of adding hints of color to monochrome, but the same results could equally be explored in a book on color photography as ways of muting color.

**Attention seeking**
*A demonstration of Paul Strand's assertion that "you pay much more attention to the subtleties of the gray scale" in a monochrome image. The color version of this view of the Bank of England is dominated by the sky and the need to hold the highlights, while a black-and-white rendering allows much more attention to be paid to the just perceptible fluting of the columns.*

Some of the most interesting photographers for me in relation to all of this are those who switched and maintained success, at least in their own eyes. Among the older and more traditional are Eliot Porter, Harry Callahan, and Joel Meyerowitz, each of whom switched to color while maintaining full respect and affection for black and white. And, if you accept black and white as normality, you could turn the question on its head and ask when and where it would be better to shoot color. This is a rather old-fashioned way of thinking, harking back to the days when color was emerging rather than dominating, but it brings a useful perspective to the same issue of choice. Edward Weston, earlier being both aloof and grumpy about color's "vulgarity" (he had conceded that "when the point of a picture subject is precisely the vulgarity… then only color film can be used validly"), finally became fascinated with the instant colors of Polaroid. He reached the not altogether surprising conclusion that "those of us who began photographing in monochrome spent years trying to avoid subject matter exciting because of its color; in this new medium, we must now seek subject matter because of its color. We must see color as form, avoiding subjects which are only 'colored' black and whites."

In many ways I think I most like Robert Frank's existential argument for monochrome, when he said, "Black and white are the colors of photography. To me they symbolize the alternatives of hope and despair to which mankind is subjected."

**Vulgarity**
*Intentional vulgarity, as Edward Weston claimed, was seen by some as the legitimate use of color in its early days.*

# BLACK & WHITE
# AS NORMALITY

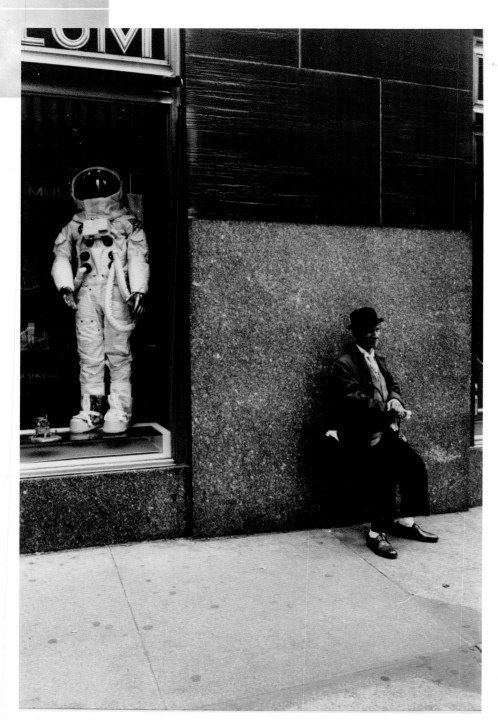

**Rockefeller**
*Joel Meyerowitz, 1970*
*Born in New York in 1938,*
*Meyerowitz began shooting*
*in 1962 and had his first*
*exhibition in 1968. He is*
*one of the masters of street*
*photography, and always*
*conscious of two distinctly*
*New York watch-words;*
*"tough," and "beautiful."*

**Roadside stand near Birmingham, 1936**
*Walker Evans*
©The Metropolitan Museum of Art, New York

# MONOCHROME IN PHOTOGRAPHY VERSUS PAINTING

The most significant difference between painting and photography is that painters have a full choice, and the decision to desaturate the palette has always been taken deliberately, whereas for photography's first century, black and white was an imposed medium. Of necessity, photographers learned to work within the restrictions of monochrome, and not surprisingly these soon ceased to be thought of as restrictions. For example, the early emulsions were sensitive principally to blue light, and in landscape photography this meant a negative properly exposed for the ground was invariably over-exposed for the sky. Good photographers learned to compose the frame to allow for blank white skies, as for example Timothy O'Sullivan.

**We began by looking at painters' experience of black and white in order to put photography in the wider context of the graphic arts.**

Another important difference between monochrome in painting and in photography is the matter of degree of color. In traditional photography there was a clear distinction between the two, because the emulsions were quite different and distinctive (of course, the situation has changed now with digital, as we will come to in Chapter 2, but the influence of photography's traditions remains strong artistically). You could do one or the other, not a version in between. No film manufacturer made "half-colorful" film. In painting, however, there has always been a wide choice of pigment, and with the exception of ink-based art, as in China, Korea, and Japan, moving towards monochrome meant a degree of desaturation

T. H. O'Sullivan. Phot.

**Black Canyon**
*Timothy O'Sullivan, 1871*
*This shot was originally*
*comissioned by Lieutennant*
*George Wheeler as part of a*
*military survey mission, and*
*has the full title "Black*
*Canyon, From Camp 8,*
*Looking Above."*

of hue that the artist could decide on the spot. In paint, there is a continuum from color to monochrome, not a binary switch, and this perhaps accounts for the relative lack of discussion by monochrome artists on this subject (Agnes Martin, for example, spoke much more about the geometry of her work than about the lack of color).

Now, digital processing offers exactly this continuum of colorfulness, so that black-and-white photography has extensions into subtlety of color rather than simply all or nothing. Any degree of saturation is possible, easily, and this brings photography closer in one aspect to painting. Being relatively new, it remains to be fully explored.

**Half-colored image**
*Digital processing makes possible the range of "colorfulness" that was formerly the preserve of painting. This interior view has been deliberately desaturated in parts.*

**Partly colored image**
*Another possibility from digital photography, which was formerly complicated with film, is to desaturate certain areas of an image, while enhancing the saturation of others.*

**Photographic quality: the silhouette**
*A Tibetan monk in the temple of Tashilhunpo, is a good example of the silhouette, invented as an art-form invented, and appropriated by photography.*

**Photographic quality: flare**
*Flare, here from specular reflections in the water of the Myakka River, Florida, is an optical effect completely characteristic of photography, but not of painting (other than painting that aims to mimic photography).*

# THE PHOTOGRAPHER'S CHOICE

Color in its earliest forms, such as Autochrome, and then the revolutionary Kodachrome, was understandably considered exotic, even threatening. But once color chemistry had matured, it was inevitable that it would take over photography almost completely.

The gradual change in the status of black-and-white photography came about as much because of how images are used and distributed as by the possibility of shooting in color. Until very recently, when photography has become fully democratic and open to almost everyone, professional and commercial needs were very influential. It was magazines in particular that were for long the means for displaying photography to a mass audience. This began in the 1930s, and lasted for at least sixty years, gradually declining in importance in the face of first television and now the internet. Color sold magazines, and the famous weeklies like Life, Stern, and Paris-Match moved quickly towards it, while monthlies like National Geographic and GEO focused all their attention on displaying the best, most exciting, and well-printed color imagery that they could find. This pushed editorial photographers to shift to color. Advertising, which filled pages on the same presses, followed immediately. Moreover, color offset printing processes became better and better, and also cheaper. As recently as the 1980s it was entirely normal for a heavily illustrated book to mix black and white in with color just for cost reasons. A signature (typically sixteen pages) of color images would frequently be followed by one of black and white. Color printing is now so efficient that today this is virtually unthinkable.

> **Viewed from the perspective of the first half of the twentieth century, it seems completely reasonable that photographers would think of black and white as normal.**

Many photographers simply moved to color and enjoyed what it had to offer. Others, as we saw, fought rearguard actions. Some simply accepted the new demands from publishers by making as few changes as possible to the way they worked. Ian Berry, a Magnum photographer, told me, "I just shoot in color as if I were using black and white [which he preferred]." For a long while, many of the avenues for displaying black-and-white photography closed off. Just the gallery print remained, which of course focused energies on print quality, in a way that color has hardly ever received.

But finally, the sheer universal availability of color, and the excesses it has been put to in richness, vibrancy, and super-saturation, have given black and white a status of refinement. The "excesses" began with the efforts of film manufacturers to satisfy their mass markets, the Japanese manufacturer Fuji being particularly active in this. They appreciated that people's memories of holiday scenes were more colorful and idealized than reality. Holiday skies, therefore, should be bluer, and this was achievable through the increasing sophistication of film technology. Printing for publication offered the same opportunities to ratchet up the colorfulness. Digital photography has unfortunately made color excess even easier, and with the broader gamut of electronic screens, the internet displays all of it.

Black and white, not surprisingly, looks all the better by comparison. Ian Jeffrey, quoted above, takes the view that "Polychrome worlds are both radiant and genial...Monochrome promised insights, visions of reality purified; or it allowed photographers freedom from the contradictory richness of full color, and a means towards emphasis and control—advantages not lightly sacrificed." Or, as Cartier-Bresson put it: "Black-and-white photography abstracts things and I like that."

## Holiday skies

*RIGHT A Velvia sky, courtesy of Fuji chemists, who recognized the desire of most holidaying photographers to reproduce blue skies as they think they should be rather than as they are.*

## Refinement

*BELOW The sidelit torso of a Khmer statue offers a classic subject for black and white, with refined treatment of the subtleties of form and texture.*

# THE PHOTOGRAPHER'S CHOICE

**38**

**Abstracting things**
*By removing color and by manipulating contrast, this view of wildebeeste on the Serengeti plains attains an abstract graphic quality, divorced from the situation itself.*

Contemporary black-and-white photography has, at least as I see it, evolved into two reasonably distinct strands. One deliberately continues the ethos of gritty documentary style; the other explores the textural, even tactile and sensual qualities of the finely crafted print. In some work, of course, the two come together briefly. This far along the historical road, decades past the introduction of a full choice between color and black and white, attitudes towards black-and-white imagery can be self-conscious. This surfaces in documentary photography, in which there is a strong feeling for continuity with the great reportage photographers of the past, such as Walker Evans, Brassaï, Henri Cartier-Bresson, Robert Capa, and others. Of course, there is also, and perhaps more importantly, the traditional argument that removing the distraction of color helps to focus attention on the meaningful activity in the scene, but the sense of following in a great tradition still pops up. Ian Jeffrey's comment that "urgent black and white" is somehow and unquestionably "apt" for serious documentary issues is typical of many thoughtful collectors, commentators, and curators. People who take photography seriously take black and white even more seriously. Consider a major recent sale, in 2008 by New York's Swann Galleries, of *Important 19th and 20th Century Photographs*. Of the 389 lots, 364 were monochrome.

**Deep sky**
*Strong geometric abstraction of an old ladder in the cliff top New Mexican settlement of Acoma. The deep blue sky was easy to convert to black with hue adjustment, for maximum contrast with the bleached wood.*

Not unexpectedly, collecting photography is biased towards safety, which favors older prints by known masters, and many people are still uncertain about the archival qualities of color prints. Nevertheless, this strongly skewed respect for monochrome prints suggests that black and white is perceived as being more serious, more at the heart of photography than mere color.

**Texture**
*The textural, tactile qualities of a black-and-white print are of prime concern—here the difference between semi-gloss and matte.*

# THE PHOTOGRAPHER'S CHOICE

## WITHOUT COLOR

Pictures without color can convey altogether different qualities to the original, which is inevitably color in the world of digitlal.

**Aland Shipbreaking**
*In the black-and-white conversion the distraction of the color is removed, allowing the eye to concentrate on the figures and the mind to consider their labors.*

**Grain sacks**
*The color original is confusing, with the red lifeboat demanding too much attention. In black and white the central protaganist is more clearly seen.*

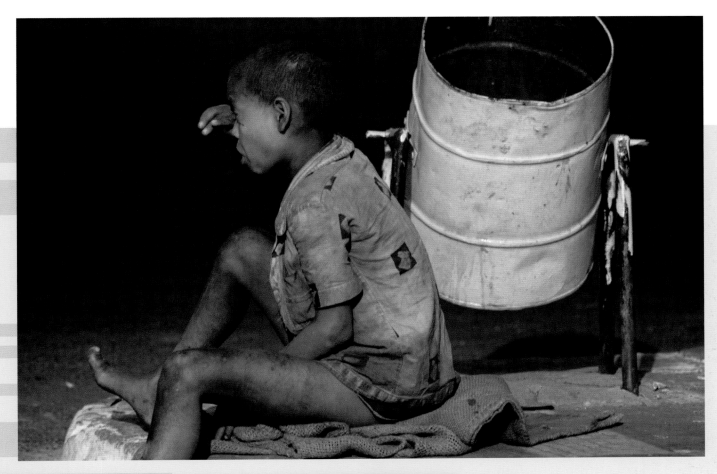

**Delhi boy**
*Black and white's reputation for "gritty reality"
suits it to reportage subjects such as these.*

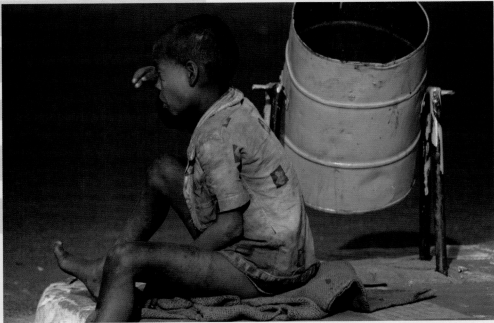

# SUBTRACTING COLOR

Color is so integral to our usual experience of the world, and of imagery, that most people (and most photographers) do not separate it in their mind's eye from everything else that is going on. In order to understand what happens when we take it away and work in monochrome, we need to know how it fits in to the total range of image qualities. Also, how it differs from the other elements in its effect.

Moreover, color elicits subjective and emotional responses in a way that other image qualities do not. Without normally analyzing it, we tend simply to like or dislike to varying degrees the way a certain color looks, or a combination of colors. The subjective response to color is powerful and pervasive, and as a result takes over viewer response to many photographs. If the color component in an image is strong, rich, unusual, or simply noticeable, there is a good chance that it will swamp the attention. Many photographers, perhaps too many, have exploited this and concentrated their energies on the power of color. Once the chemistry of color film was properly established in the early 1960s, the opportunity to concentrate on it as an image quality began to be exploited by a number of photographers. One of the most influential was the Swiss Ernst Haas, who notably exploited the strong but dark color saturation that Kodachrome gave when slightly underexposed. By contrast Eliot Porter worked with a more restrained palette, but still with a sensual approach in which the colors themselves are often the principal reason for the photograph.

And because color triggers emotional responses, there is also usually an unquestioned assumption that it works on a scale of beauty, or at least attractiveness. To say "what a spectacular sunset," or "look at how blue the water is," or "that gray really sets off the pink," or any of the many other common value judgments on color, is to acknowledge that the effect of color can be likeable—and for most people should be likeable. This gut reaction to color is by far the most common, and in this way it stands apart from the other formal graphic elements, which we'll now examine. There are a number of ways of sub-dividing the graphic components of an image, but the most generally accepted is: point, line, shape, texture, and color. In the way that these are used and interact, there is contrast, balance, and dynamics (or vectors). Subtracting color enhances those remaining. In practice this means that the components and qualities most affected are the graphic ones of shape, the graphic structure of the image, and the gradation along the gray tonal scale, as well as the three-dimensional ones of volume and texture.

**At the risk of oversimplifying, subtracting color from imagery allows the other graphic elements and dynamics to increase in importance. Indeed, compels them to, like a sort of Boyle's Law of attention— fewer components in an image expand to engage the attention of the viewer.**

**Ruins**

*In this image taken in the abandoned Khmer ruin of Banteay Chhmar, with its inimitable face-tower, the color version distracts without adding any particular value, while a black-and-white rendering pulls attention back to where it was intended—on the face-tower.*

## Abu Shouk
LEFT A Sudanese woman from Darfur, recently arrived in a refugee camp after her husband was killed in an attack on their village. Arguably, the bright colors favored by all Sudanese women detracts from the severity of the situation.

## Tianluokeng tulous
BELOW By careful use of hue adjustment, the focus of attention can be shifted. In the color original, the green of the rice fields is quite dominant. A straight conversion to black and white if anything lessens the prominence of these unique Hakka communal dwellings. Hue adjustment that lightens yellow and green, however, raises the key and increases the visual weight of the buildings.

# SHAPE

There are, in fact, two intimately related issues here. Shape in photography can be pushed in two directions. One is toward the two-dimensional and graphic—"pure" shapes that behave as cutouts, as in a strong silhouette.

The other is toward creating the impression of volume, roundedness, and three dimensions. In either case, the emphasis is on formal graphic structure. As Joel Meyerowitz, another photographer who moved from black and white to color, put it, "it was a big step to cut off black-and-white work and commit myself to color. You're really changing the nature of your response. It's a very different game out there. Black and white has more form. Somehow pictures look like there's a compressed formal structure running through them, tying events together. In color there's more of a languid flow from one thing to the other. Learning how to make that switch was a departure for me."

In fact, although here I'm isolating the particularly black-and-white qualities of photography, beginning with shape, they are all interconnected. Shape can be used to define form, although not necessarily. This in turn gives a sense of volume and presence, which we'll see a few pages further on. Shape depends heavily on outline, and in photography this is defined by edge contrast, as opposed to in drawing, where lines are more normal. This contrast in itself draws more attention to edge transitions in monochrome than in color, with all the attendant issues of sharpness, smooth gradation in the case of a soft or defocused edge, and possible artifacts such as halos when you apply sharpening.

**Silhouette shape**
*Shape based on the edges of a silhouette is clear, graphic, and two-dimensional. While the sunset colors are fairly attractive, this is nevertheless a candidate for black and white because of these graphic qualities. And the removal of color further keeps the attention on the outline of these old Shanghai roofs.*

**Either way**
*An image, in Iceland, that works perfectly well in color or black and white, though differently. The black and white is arguably stronger, at least when processed this way for good contrast, with the shape of the fencing and white church emphasized.*

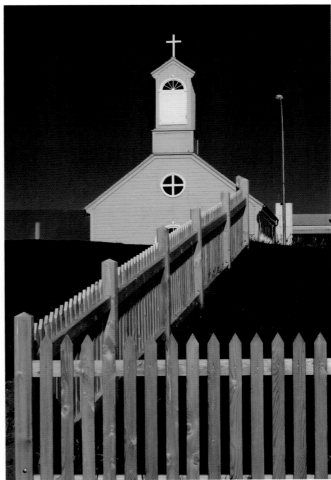

**Limits of shape**
*A cropped detail from a larger image showing two ill effects from over-sharpening (in the right-hand image). One of these is haloing around the edges, particularly noticeable around the horse's ears; the other is an exaggeration of noise in the shadows of the horse and rider.*

# STRUCTURE

Picture situations that contain a strong potential for structure notably include elements of line and shape, almost always heightened by some form of contrast. These conditions, and the images here are just two of countless examples, create what Henri Cartier-Bresson described as the "geometry" of a photograph when he said, "I think of what I see, and the geometry, that means everything has to be composed properly." He also wrote of composing as appreciating "...the beauty of the form; that is, a geometry awakened by what's offered."

**Composition in photography can be subtly embedded, so that the viewer is unaware of it, but it can also be strongly evident, and this depends on two things: whether or not the photographer wants to push this particular graphic aspect of the image, and the opportunities that the scene offers.**

Black and white enhances these possibilities by taking away the distraction of color and forcing attention more on the contrast across edges, as the two examples here show. In the case of the interior of the Guggenheim Museum by Frank Lloyd Wright, the interior is not particularly colorful, but even so the differences in color from the mixed lighting contribute nothing to the image and simply serve to distract. In black and white, the image is stronger and cleaner. In the other image, under a hill farmer's house in southern China, the wooden construction, the relationship between calf and buffalo, and the exaggeration of all of this by using a wide-angle lens (at 27mm focal length), creates the potential for pronounced geometry. Again, however, the cool-warm color contrast works across this. Here, careful processing made the most of the structure, and we will look at this in detail later, on page 154.

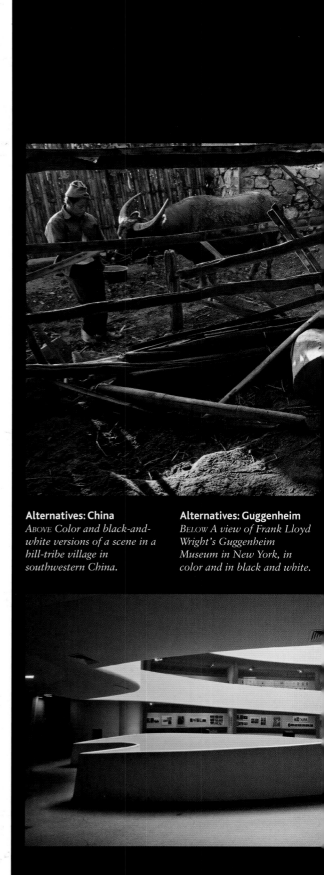

**Alternatives: China**
*Above Color and black-and-white versions of a scene in a hill-tribe village in southwestern China.*

**Alternatives: Guggenheim**
*Below A view of Frank Lloyd Wright's Guggenheim Museum in New York, in color and in black and white.*

THE BLACK & WHITE TRADITION

# TONAL NUANCE

**P**hysiologically, our visual system responds more sensitively to some hues than to others, which is why yellows and yellow-greens are brighter to our eyes. But more than this, there is our psychological response to different hues. One simple example of this is that "hot" colors around orange are readily associated with flame and burning, and so the production of light. Most people feel these to be inherently brighter than, say, blues, which we tend to associate with water, coolness, and dim light. Further proof is the huge choice in translating hues into tones when you use one of the various software processing methods that mixes channels (as demonstrated opposite, and we will see in considerably more detail in Chapter 3).

Take this away, and the tonal scale simplifies dramatically. What this allows is a clearer, purer concentration on the subtleties of transition between shades of gray. Immediately, as you would expect,

**This is a very specific photographic concern, by its nature subtle and personal. If you study the examples here with some care, you can see how complex the issue of brightness can be in a color image.**

this places great importance on the smoothness of tonal gradients, such as in a clear sky. Unevenness, and in particular banding, is even more apparent with no color to distract the attention. Long smooth gradients show up the efficiency of the sensor, and make 16-bit-per-channel processing a priority.

On a more subjective level, there is extra room to play with tonal transitions in different areas of the scale. You might, for example, want delicacy in the upper mid tones in particular, or very finely tunes hints of detail in deep shadow areas. All of this naturally leads to different interpretations of tone which, as we'll see in a few pages, has a wider range of acceptable results in monochrome than in color.

I mentioned channel mixing in software monochrome conversion, which you would do as part of your Raw processing (providing that you shot Raw) but which can also be performed on TIFFs. This, of course, adds another and very large dimension to controlling tonal nuance. It makes it possible to achieve almost any conceivable distribution of tones, with almost too much choice. It certainly demands a clear idea of what you want to achieve, ideally before you begin the process.

**Morning sun**
*Early morning sun just beginning to filter through fog creates an atmospheric distribution of tone in this image of boathouses. Preserving delicate tonal transitions is essential to the success of a picture like this.*

# RESTORING LOST NUANCE

There are circumstances in which color tells a story very quickly.
With a little thought, however, that can be achieved in mono too.

Color

Desautrated

Tonal distinction preserved

| BLACK AND WHITE | |
| --- | --- |
| REDS | 99% |
| YELLOWS | 88% |
| GREENS | 40% |
| CYANS | -193% |
| BLUES | -48% |
| MAGENTAS | 80% |

*In color, this image of gold smelting clearly stresses the intensity of the flames, whereas a straight desaturation loses the sense completely. Recovering the tonal distinction involves operating the sliders in hue adjustment to darken the man's protective suit and brighten the orange flames.*

### Banding
*A regular issue in digital processing especially when the adjustments are significant, is banding across smooth gradations. Some people argue that the removal of color, as in this Utah landscape, focuses attention more closely on faults such as this.*

# VOLUME & FORM

**H**elmut and Alison Gernsheim, in their classic A Concise History of Photography put the issue of shape and form succinctly when they wrote that "In monochrome the massing of light and shade and the reproduction of texture are of the utmost importance," making the comparison with color photography. We'll deal with texture on the following pages, but for many black-and-white photographers, this massing that uses brightness is the key concern in technique. Eliot Porter, who began in black and white but made his reputation in color, was unequivocal when he wrote that, "When photographing subjects like rocks, the approach is entirely different, because in black and white you see the forms much more than you do in color."

**Form and volume both play an important part in revealing each other, with texture key to the viewer's understanding of the picture.**

**Precious Wendletrap**
LEFT *With diffused lighting from the left and a reflector on the right, against black velvet, the setting, lighting, and processing for this still-life of a Precious Wendletrap have been chosen primarily with a view to emphasizing the volume of the shell, so that we can sense its three-dimensionality and delicacy.*

**Bronze statue**
RIGHT *Side-lighting, a hint of secondary lighting from behind and left, and a low-key treatment combine to stress the form of this ancient Khmer bronze statue.*

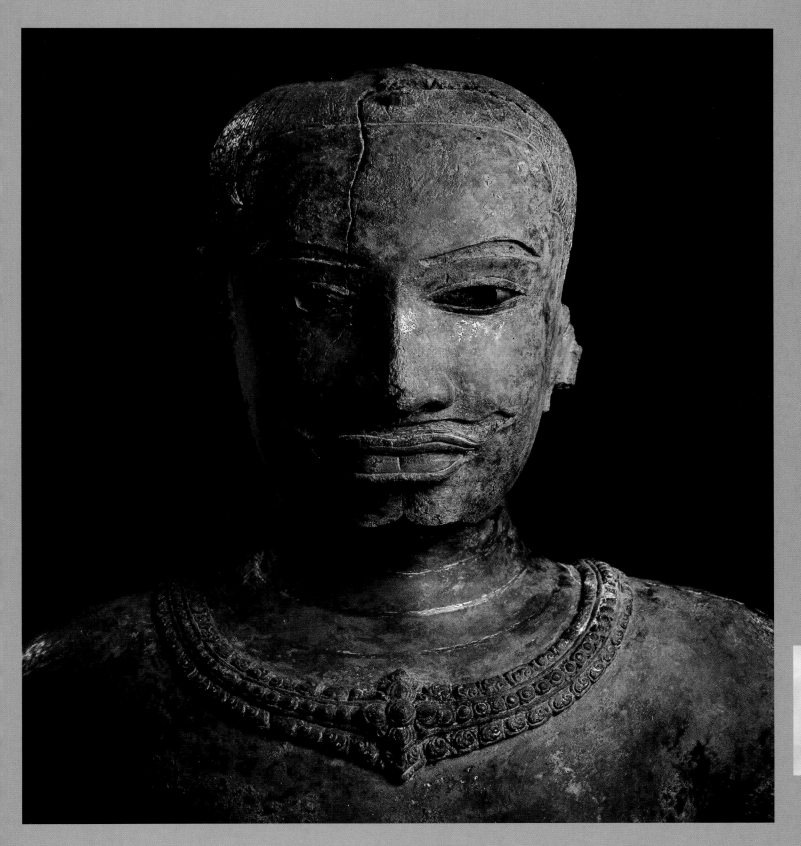

# TEXTURE

A pebble-dashed wall, to give an example, has a particular consistency of roughness and spacing. The reason why texture becomes a more prominent, malleable quality in black and white than in color is—as we've already seen for shape and form—removing color from the equation makes the presentation of texture a pure exercise in tonal modulation.

The simple way of treating texture in a photograph is in terms of its strength, and almost any relief texture looks stronger under a point-source light that casts hard shadows, and in particular under raking light, from a low angle. But really, this is not just simple but simplistic. There is an infinite variety of texture, including smooth glosses and metallic sheens, and the key to handling texture is to connect it to the object whose surface it covers, and what you want to say about it in the image. If, for example, a ceramic vase or bowl has a pronounced and gritty texture, how much do you want to stress this aspect of it rather than the volume? Almost certainly there will have to be a compromise. These kinds of possibilities and decisions are endless, and there are certainly no rights or wrongs. The place you give to texture in an image is entirely your choice—in as much as you have control over the lighting which, ultimately, reveals texture.

**Texture is structure and form on a small scale, meaning small relative to the view. And, because a texture is, by definition, something that is reasonably consistent over a substantial area of a surface, it is usually a repetitive structure.**

**Braces**
*Another lighting technique to reveal texture is this—a large, diffused area light aimed from in front of the camera but out of frame. This lit the entire stone slab on which these old braces were placed, while showing its texture.*

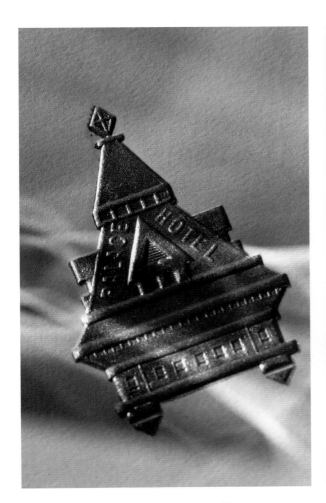

### Badrutts

*The metallic texture of an embossed letterhead in silver called for a variety of light falling on it to convey its texture. The solution was a spotlight aimed through an empty wine glass to throw caustics over the close-up, plus strong fill from a reflector on the right.*

### Badrutts silverware

*Hotel silverware in close-up. The texture in this case includes lettering and symbol that need to read clearly. The answer is an area light, but not so large that its reflection swamps the entire curve of the metal.*

# TEXTURE

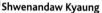

**Shwenandaw Kyaung**

NEAR RIGHT *Texture on a medium-close-up scale, of weathered wood carvings in the teak wall of an old Burmese palace in Mandalay. The cross-lighting from a low sun reveals this texture perfectly.*

**Real Alcazar**

FAR RIGHT *Overlaid on the texture of the old wall—in the Real Alcazar in Seville—is a second graphic texture of dappled shadows. Again, lighting at an angle to the surface helps predictably.*

**Orange pearl**

LEFT *Sometimes texture is best revealed with diffused light, as here, of a rare pearl nestling among black pebbles. The gaps in the stones create shadow, but the delicate glossy sphere is unaffected by highlights.*

**Soft light**

OPPOSITE *Totally shadowless lighting from an overcast day allows the naturally contrasting textures of the round art piece and rusted iron to assert themselves. The subjects need no help from traditional sidelighting.*

# INTERPRETATION

**One theme running through this book—running through my mind, really—is that monochrome, by being distanced from what we take in through our eyes, allows more extreme manipulation without breaching any norms of acceptability.**

et me expand on this a little. Color photography, despite coming late in the twentieth century to the photographic world, carries with it, automatically, the presumption of being close to reality. It's expected in most instances. Or rather, it's unquestioned. Make major alterations to a color image, such as hue changes, selective changes, and they will very definitely look like alterations. Adjustments at the same level of intrusion in black and white, however, are accorded much more latitude by most viewers.

We'll come to the large-scale possibilities later, in Chapter 2 when we look at processing, but for now let's limit ourselves to three moves that are both basic and common to both color and monochrome. These are tonal compression, brightness, and global contrast. The argument is that you can push each of these acceptably to a more extreme degree in monochrome than in color. Any judgments here are subjective, of course—a matter of taste—so it's perhaps better that I'm not didactic here. Better to let the examples speak for themselves. Tonal compression means clipping at either or both ends of the scale, which is usually more acceptable for the shadows because of the long photographic tradition of the silhouette, much less so for the highlights. Even so, it can work perfectly well for a black-and-white image. Altering brightness is basically a change of key (between high-key and low-key), which we explore in more detail on pages 158-165. Global, as opposed to local, contrast affects the entire image, while the ends of the scale remain fixed, and are traditionally altered by applying a classic S-curve or reverse S-curve.

## STAGES OF INTERPRETATION

Creating the perfect black-and-white image can involve a number of stages, including—as here—the use of masks to target specific areas for different tonal treatment.

**Dobi wallah**
*The color original, of yellow cloths drying on the banks of the Ganges at Varanasi.*

**Desaturated**
*A straight desaturation across all channels, purely for reference. All sense of contrast in the cloths has been lost.*

| REDS | 45% |
| YELLOWS | 125% |
| GREENS | 294% |
| CYANS | -79% |
| BLUES | -198% |
| MAGENTAS | 80% |

| AMOUNT | +25 |
| darken | lighten |
| MIDPOINT | +79 |

### Black & White Settings 1

*Using hue adjustment, I aim for a contrast that will have the cloths light and the river dark; raising yellows and greens, lowering blues and cyan. This certainly achieves contrast, but vignetting that was present is exaggerated. Also, both the cloth highlights and the dark shadows in the upper half need tempering.*

### Black & White Settings 2

*Using Lens Correction in Photoshop, the vignetting, most prominent in the upper corners, is reduced.*

### Black & White Settings 3

*To darken the foreground overall while increasing its contrast, a mask is roughly painted over this area with a large soft brush. The curve shown here is then applied. Some unintended darkening has occurred at left and right because of the mask's imprecision.*

INTERPRETATION

59

### Black & White Settings 5

*The next step is to heighten contrast in the river, with its boats, to get a gritty feel. The river area is selected by mask painting as above, intentionally leaving a gap in the middle of the right-hand boats, which are already very dark. A strong contrast-creating S-curve is applied. Now, some unevenness across the water has crept in, leaving the top left and right corners of the image too dark.*

### Black & White Settings 4

*These two small dark areas are restored with the History Brush.*

### Black & White Settings 6

*To lighten the corners, they are mask-painted, and then a curve applied. Note that only the upper part of the range is lightened—the dark shadows are held in place. This is the final image—clearly just one interpretation of several possible ones.*

# LIMITS OF COLOR

What we have done above in black and white is to make strong, even extreme, adjustments to the image as shot. Now I want to show the limits of adjustment if we were to work in color.

### Color Settings 1
*These limits are much tighter. First, let's apply 100% Vibrance (which is, by its design, less extreme than the same Saturation increase would be). Even then the result has already gone beyond what most people would consider reasonable.*

**VIBRANCE**

| | |
|---|---|
| VIBRANCE | +100 |
| SATURATION | 0 |

### Color Settings 2
*If instead we decide to shift all the hues, there is even less latitude. Here 15%, which is very little, is about as far as we could go and maintain some semblance of naturalism.*

**HUE/SATURATION**

| | |
|---|---|
| HUE | +15 |
| SATURATION | 0 |
| LIGHTNESS | 0 |

**PHOTO FILTER**

FILTER: Warming Filter (85)

DENSITY      50 %

☑ Preserve Luminosity

### Color Settings 3
*Finally, let's see how strong a standard filter we can apply and still seem natural. This is a basic warming filter, and the overcast light might suggest it. But applied at 50% we have quite a different effect, almost like a colored monochrome! The lesson from these three color experiments is clear—black and white lends itself to greater extremes of processing interpretation than does color.*

# FILM QUALITIES

**The particular look of film has been around long enough to be an established part of our cultural understanding of the image, even if it is no longer present in many of the pictures that we are presented with. It carries with it certain expectations of truth.**

Every medium adds its own internal qualities to an image, be it oil paint, charcoal, watercolor, or film. And for photography, emulsions, both film and paper, have dominated it for so long that their particular characteristics are embedded in its language. Consider the history of black-and-white emulsions. Over the course of the late nineteenth century and most of the twentieth century, many monochrome film emulsions were invented, each with a different quality, varying by a mix of grain and texture, contrast, tonal structure, and other things that was hard to pin down but nevertheless made most of them identifiable.

Graininess in film is caused by silver particles clumping. In fact, when people talk about grain in film, they usually mean much larger structures, as individual grains are normally impossible to see at normal viewing distances. This goes back to the structure of an emulsion, in which silver halide crystals are suspended in a matrix. They react latently (meaning not at the point of exposure) to light falling on the film, and processing converts these exposed crystals into black silver. That, skipping the details, is the essence. The silver halide is the active ingredient in film, in the form of a mass of crystals distributed as evenly as possible in the gelatin layer that makes up the body of an emulsion. The size and distribution of these crystals, also known commonly as grains, varies according to the type of film, but in an average emulsion each measures about 1/1000th of a millimeter across. The silver and halide components are held together in a lattice arrangement by electrical bonds; when the photons strike, they disrupt the electrical status quo by adding energy to the crystal.

One of the special qualities of film, lost in digital sensors, is that it responds to brightness in a way that is quite similar to the human eye. Basically, it can handle a wide range of brightness (dynamic range, in other words) by compressing its response. Put more practically, it means that as more light falls on the film, the emulsion responds more sluggishly.

Most of the improvements and alterations that film manufacturers used to make to their products had to do with the size and shape of these grains and the way in which they are suspended in the emulsion. To make a film more sensitive to light, a greater area of each affected grain needs to be exposed. Traditionally, this was done by using larger grains, but a more modern

## FILM STRUCTURE

In a typical black-and-white film, the emulsion is a layer of gelatin in which the light sensitive crystals of silver bromide are embedded. This is supported on a tough, stable base, usually cellulose acetate. A scratch-resistant coating protects the emulsion and an antihalation layer prevents stray light from being reflected back into the emulsion from below.

Light sensitive crystals

Scratch-resistant coating

Gelatin

Adhesive

Cellulose-acetate base

Adhesive

Antihalation backing

development is to use grains that are flatter rather than lumpy; if they lay flat-side towards the light, the effect is greater sensitivity without more silver halide bulk. Film with larger, or flatter, grains reacts more readily to light and is therefore "faster." However, the price that has to be paid for this increase in film speed is a coarser image, more so with large-grain than with flat-grain technology. The increased granularity gives rise to a grainier appearance, which in the very fastest films or with great enlargement actually breaks up the image into a pronounced speckled texture.

To maximize image quality, film manufacturers set smaller grains into a thinner emulsion, so as to reduce the internal reflections that degrade the image in a thick layer of gelation. This type of emulsion has a fine-grained appearance but reacts less well to light and is therefore "slow." The improved sensitivity of flat grains is also used in combination with cubic grains for fine-grained emulsions that can produce exceptionally sharp images. Even distribution of the crystals and a fine internal structure contribute to this.

**Shadow detail**
*Another view of a negative—here 6×6 cm—reveals detail in the coat of this Bactrian camel even in a dark silhouette.*

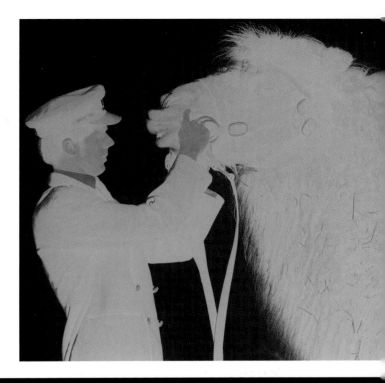

**Judging negative then print**
*Black-and-white printing from negatives demanded experience to be able to "see" the image from its tonally reversed negative.*

# FILM QUALITIES

### Highlight roll-off
*BELOW Even shooting straight into a bright sun in a clear day, film handles the excessive contrast quite gently in the highlights. The tones roll off gradually towards the solid white of the sun, with no obvious banding.*

### Ruby beach negative
*RIGHT A negative, which on examination always shows more detail than a straight silver print can deliver, gives an even better demonstration of roll-off.*

The net result of all this effort is that different film emulsions have different styles of graininess, and many photographers who are wedded to film feel able to discriminate between brands. How real this is matters less than that film photographers certainly used to favor the grain structure of certain films, and generally learned to appreciate this quality. Kodak's Tri-X was always well-regarded for this. Philosophically you could argue that even though film manufacturers have always tried to minimize the appearance of grain, it remains structurally a part of the process and of the image, and so should be accepted and even loved for that reason. There are certainly many examples in black and white of photographers emphasizing and using this quality.

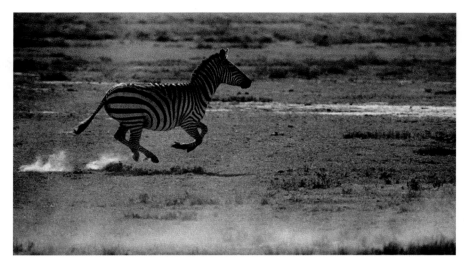

**Tri-X**
*Tri-X in magnification, shows the distinct and definite grain structure prized and enjoyed by many film photographers.*

**Birds**
*George Krause, 1965. This is a photograph that relies heavily on revealing the grain in order to create what the photographer calls "an image that suggested a Seurat pointillist drawing or an intaglio aquatint." To this end he exaggerated the effect by later applying Victor's Mercury Intensifier. Krause, a renowned printer as well as photographer, has since moved happily to digital black and white.*

# FILM QUALITIES

There is also a paradoxical relationship between graininess and sharpness. Sharpness is a subjective quality, to which the measurable quality of resolution contributes only partly. Other things come into play, including contrast, and sharpness is very much a matter of judgment, as becomes immediately obvious when people discuss it. "Not sharp enough" and "too sharp" or "over-sharpened" are clearly expressions of taste. At a degree of enlargement when it becomes visible, and especially with high-speed and pushed film, grain can act to help sharpness. Even though overall the less noticeable the grain, the sharper an image looks, in its detail, graininess with a precise structure can, just by giving a definable texture to the image, provide a different kind of sharpness.

However, grain in color film is not the same thing. To begin with, at a microscopic level the crisp black silver of black and white is replaced with a rather fuzzier dye cloud. Then, a tri-pack color emulsion has more depth, with overlapping color dye-clouds adding to the softness. What is visible in a high-speed black-and-white film image as a crisp structure becomes more amorphous in fast color film. One different monochrome process borrows some of color film's technology. In such "chromogenic" films, the original silver is removed after the first development, and replaced with a dye. The result is a virtual absence of the traditional grainy texture, which was not a foregone advantage for the reasons discussed above.

Interestingly, some image processing software manufacturers have cottoned on to this latent desire among photographers to recreate the look of traditional films, and in particular their graininess. The result is pre-sets that make an image look as if it were shot on a specific brand of film. The examples here are from DxO Optics.

## FILM GRAIN DIGITALLY

In these examples, DxO Film Pack, a software processing application, offers measured simulations of a selection of 50 films, not just the grain characteristics, but the characteristic curve response. As the company puts it, this is from "modeling the colorimetric responses of silver-halide films. For the modeling process, great care was taken in the development of these films, which was entrusted to major professional laboratories in Paris and New York."

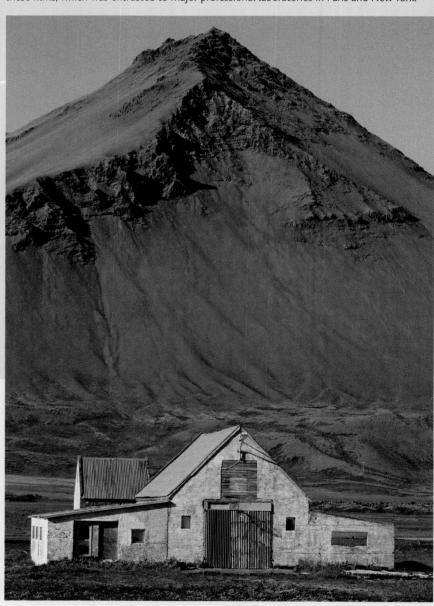

THE BLACK & WHITE TRADITION

DxO Agfa APX 25

DxO HP5 Plus 400

DxO Kodak HIE

DxO T-Max 3200

# SECTION 2
# DIGITAL MONOCHROME

**W**hile digital photography is for the most part practised in color, camera sensors are strictly monochrome. But of course, so is film. Both react to the quantity of light, and not to sections of the visible spectrum. And both need a process of color separation in order to record and reproduce the colors of the world. In the case of sensors, the near-universal method is a grid of colored filters—red, green, and blue—attached to the front of the sensor. The alternative is the Foveon sensor, in which three layers—blue at the top, then green, then red—are stacked, on the same principle used by tri-pack color film.

Black-and-white photography with a digital camera, therefore, is something of a retro operation, as the color information needs to be removed. However, far from being a disadvantage, the color information can be put to excellent use in allowing the brightness of any color to be adjusted as you convert it to a shade of gray.

For anyone coming to this from black-and-white film photography, there are several key differences. First, camera sensors react to light in proportion to how much strikes each individual photo-site, while film has a generous latitude that causes it to be more forgiving of over-exposure, and to some extent under-exposure. In a digital exposure, the sudden loss of highlights from a slight miscalculation and over-exposure is always a concern. The camera sensor has two critical limits: highlight loss, or clipping as it is known, at the top end, and noise at the other end in the shadows.

Much of this chapter is devoted to hue adjustment. This is the post-processing stage in which you can choose and fine-tune the brightness relationship between different colors in any scene. The blue of the sky, for example, can be lightened or darkened independently of the overall exposure, simply by adjusting a blue or a cyan slider. The technical side is straightforward; much more interesting is deciding when and why to use these powerful controls.

# THE MONOCHROME SENSOR

In order to extract the color information from a scene, the total light reaching the sensor needs to be filtered in some way. Filtering simply means blocking some wavelengths in order to allow others through, and the standard method for almost all camera sensors is the Bayer array, a mosaic filter manufactured with a pattern of red, green, and blue. Each photosite is filtered with one or the other,

**Like film, and every other photographic process before it, camera sensors respond to total light, not color.**

and the standard arrangement has twice the number of green filters than red or blue, in an attempt to match the sensitivity of the human eye, which has its peak response to yellow-green wavelengths.

This arrangement means that the color information is much less than the light information, and the camera's processor uses interpolation to guess the mix of color for each pixel. In practice, this works perfectly well, even though it sounds crude, but to get back to monochrome, the colors need to be desaturated. This is indeed what happens in cameras that offer the option of monochrome—a straight desaturation of each of the three channels: red, green, and blue.

The hidden advantage of shooting color when you really want black and white is that later, when you come to process the images on the computer, this color information can be used to vary the brightness of specific hues. For more on this extraordinarily valuable feature of digital capture, see Colors into Tones, page 106, and the pages following.

In theory, another way of shooting in black and white would be to have a monochrome sensor—that is, without the Bayer array in front of it. Kodak indeed once did produce such a camera, the DCS 760M, but it was a short-lived experiment. The argument for this is simply that the resolution and contrast will be better without the Bayer array, and a convincing demonstration for this is presented by Lloyd Chambers on http://diglloyd.com/diglloyd/2007-07-blog.html. The practical argument against is that there is simply insufficient demand for a mono-only camera.

## RGB CHANNELS

When an image is viewed in terms of its channels only, it's easy to see how black-and-white photography can benefit from treating each channel separately.

**Bayer filter**
*In the Bayer filter bonded to the front of most camera sensors, alternating red, green and blue each filters cover one photosite. The color resolution is thus much lower than the spatial resolution.*

**Red Cow**

*In this strongly colored image of a bull sculpture in Chicago, the green and blue channels almost completely block the red.*

**Blue channel**

**Red channel**

**Green channel**

# LINEAR CAPTURE

**L**inear capture, depending on your view, is in essence a technical matter that has already been addressed. Now, suddenly, that makes it seem puzzling and arcane, and indeed most photographers never even see a linear result. Nevertheless at some point, especially when we are delving deeply into the digital process, it needs to be dealt with and understood.

**The idea of linear capture arrived new to photography with digital. Because film responds differently to light than does a digital sensor, the matter was of no relevance before.**

Basically, linear in the context of photography means a straightforward, one-to-one response to light. This is what a sensor does. It counts the photons, photosite by photosite, and delivers a signal that corresponds exactly to the numbers. That sounds uncomplicated, basic, and normal, but it is not the way that we perceive light. Nor is it the way that film responds. Both the eye and film react to light in a very non-linear way. They compress the information, with the very significant advantage that they can sense a wider range of brightness than they would otherwise. This compression effect, essentially a log scale of sensing rather than linear, affects other senses as well. If you hold a 100-gram (3½ ounces) weight in your hand, then add a second, the combination feels less than the full 200 grams. The same applies to sound—twice as loud actually seems less.

Because this is the way we see, any imaging system that plans to deliver realistic looking photographs has to conform to the eye's non-linear processes. Film, fortunately and mainly coincidentally, has a similar built in compression. In practice, this means that highlights recorded on film don't just disappear suddenly into blank whiteness, but hold up quite well. In a landscape view in which the sky, for example, shades from a light gray cloud to the intense brightness of the sun, black-and-white negative film will capture more than you might expect. And the same goes for the shadows.

A Raw digital image, however, does not work like this. For a start, most of the bits used to encode the capture are devoted to the brighter end of the register

## GAMMA

The term gamma is used often in computing and in describing digital images. When applied to monitor screens, it is a measure of the relationship between voltage input and the brightness intensity, and because of the way a computer display works, a Raw, uncorrected digital image would look darker and more contrasty than our eyes would find normal. To compensate for this, gamma correction is applied inside the camera after capture, as the exercise will help you to understand. The typical gamma correction curve shown here has the effect of making an image brighter (because most of it is shifted to the left) and less contrasty (because of its shape, which lifts dark tones more than light ones).

**Gamma Variation**
*The effects of lowering and raising the gamma.*

Gamma lower

Gamma higher

rather than the more visually useful mid-tones. A Raw histogram, as shown in the example here, looks strange to anyone used to working with histograms in, say, Photoshop, with most of the values squeezed to the left. Secondly, as brightness marches in step with the photons counted, there is none of the gentle roll-off in the highlights that happens with film. In an area of an image that shades from bright to white, there is a sudden break point and a resulting edge that looks unpleasantly artificial.

Because of this, digitally captured photographs always need to be adjusted with what is called a gamma correction. A typical one is shown here, and in effect

it brightens the shadow areas while tailing off towards the highlights. The camera applies one of these when it processes the image just shot into a JPEG or TIFF. If you shoot Raw, the preview you see on the camera's LCD screen is actually taken from a JPEG. One of the most convincing arguments for shooting in Raw format is that the processing power of your computer combined with the sophistication of image processing software far exceeds that available in the confines of the camera's processing system.

## GAMMA CORRECTION

**Gamma correction**
*A typical gamma correction curve as applied in the camera to bring the image to an appearance that seems normal to our eyes.*

**Linear Process**
*The linear capture as it would appear without normal in-camera processing, with the accompanying histogram in which most of the tones are crowded to the left.*

# THE CLIPPING PROBLEM

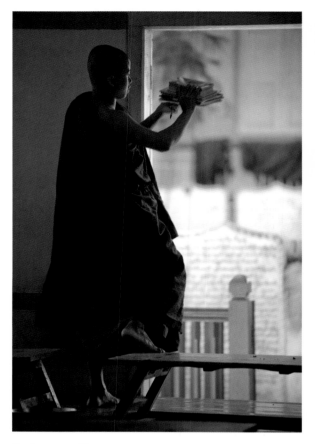

**Final recovered image**

The problem of clipping much more important for the appearance of the image, and especially in the highlights. An all-too-common result is a bright highlight ending up looking like a blank white patch with hard edges. It is debatable whether this looks worse in color or in black and white, but the argument for being especially careful in monochrome is that tonal gradation receives more visual attention when there is no color to distract.

**As just explained, one of the problematic features of digital capture is that the brightness captured in the image is directly related to the exposure, and does not, as with film and the human eye, diminish at the upper and lower ends of the scale.**

Imagine a scene in which there is a steady increase in brightness across part of the frame, as in, say, a sky looking towards the sun, or a studio set-up in which a softened light shades across a plain white background. The latter is easy enough to create and test. What we want to see is a smooth, steady progression from mid-tones towards an almost-white. Given care with the exposure, this is easy enough to achieve shooting film, and even if the brightest point is actually a featureless white, the transition towards it will at least be smooth and appear acceptable. This is because the film's response to increasing exposure slows down. On the S-shaped response curve that used to be familiar to photographers working with film, we have here reached the shoulder. Film's diminishing response to bright light produces a gentle roll-off towards maximum brightness.

With a digital image, this is difficult. Moving towards the highlight, what typically happens is that the tones shade normally up to a point, and then suddenly change to featureless white. Hence the apt term "clipping" used to describe the sudden loss of values in digital highlights. The effect, as you can see here in the example, is an edge, which is unrealistic and definitely unwanted. The only way to avoid this is to reduce the exposure to the point at which there is no clipping, meaning for the highlights. If the contrast range in the scene is high, or even normal, this creates problems in the shadow areas, which will be underexposed.

The other solution is in the processing, or afterwards. One of the saving graces of shooting color in order to arrive at black and white is that the different response of the three channels, red, green, and blue, can work to the advantage of recovering clipped highlights. Usually, the three channels respond differently to exposure, meaning that it is unlikely that they all clip at exactly the same point. As long as at least one channel retains some information, there is a chance to interpolate from that. Highlight recovery, a notable feature of Raw converters, attempts to reconstruct the detail information in a clipped channel from the other two, or even in two clipped channels from the third.

# CLIPPING WARNING AND REPAIR

### Death Valley dunes
*A film image, straight into the sun, in which the shading towards total overexposure near the sun is gradual.*

### Highlight clipping
*By contrast to the Death Valley picture, a digital into-the-sun image shows a sharp break at the level where clipping (over-exposure) begins. Holding down the ⌥/ Alt key in Photoshop Levels while dragging the slider reveals this dramatically.*

### Characteristic film response curve
*The so-called characteristic curve of a film, showing how the response to light deviates in the shadows and highlights—at both ends the response gradually weakens, which has the effect of compressing dark and light areas.*

### Camera Raw warning
*Processing the raw file, the red patches show clipped highlights before attempting to recover them.*

### Clipped
*Clipped highlights from normal processing, revealed in the histogram, which shows these crowded against the right side.*

### Using the Recovery slider
*The Recovery slider rebuilds highlight information by using information that survives in one or more channels. Here it is used at 75% (up from 0), and the warning areas are almost completely gone.*

# NOISE, BIT DEPTH, & SHADING

**In the days of film, grain structure used to receive a great deal of attention from black-and-white photographers in particular, and now is probably the time to look at the perceptual and even philosophical differences between grain and noise.**

At first thought noise and grain appear to have much in common. Both are artifacts in that they interfere with the image. They handicap it and hold back detail and tone. But film photographers saw grain differently from the way in which digital photographers regard noise. Noise is mainly a sampling error—not enough photons reaching parts of the sensor from dark areas of the scene. There are other, less important causes, to do with sensor design and performance, but the overall effect is that at high sensitivity and long exposures, pixel values are not consistent as they ought to be; instead they vary and produce a blotchy, gritty result.

Grain, on the other hand, is generally considered a more acceptable image characteristic, as we saw on pages 62-67. First, it is embedded in the medium and is an integral part of the image-making process. Second, it has a distinct structure which can, with certain films, add a pleasing texture. This effect does not happen with digital noise, which, like hiss and crackle in a poor audio transmission, is simply evidence of a weak signal. Taste, of course, is an individual matte, but it is hard to imagine promoting the visual appeal of noise. One of black and white's advantages over color is that only luminance noise needs to be dealt with, not color noise, and the absence of color artefacts makes the overall effect less unpleasant.

Unlike grain, however, noise can be treated. There are several kinds and causes of noise, but by far the most common in most photography is associated with high ISO sensitivity settings. The amount of noise at different ISO settings varies from camera to camera, and depends very much on the sensor design. In particular, larger individual photosites are likely to suffer less from noise because they can collect more photons. Efficient Raw processing, particularly at the early, de-mosaicing stage, also makes a difference. And, the appearance of noise can be reduced, even sometimes eliminated, by post-processing. This last is by no means a perfect solution, however, as it tackles the effect, not the root cause, and there is always a trade-off between reducing the noise and an over-smooth, plastic-like appearance.

Closely related is the issue of smooth tonal gradation—and making changes to smooth tones. Just as favoring the blue channel when making a black-and-white conversion tends to enhance the appearance of noise, editing changes such as contrast curves also run the risk of creating artifacts. In particular, there is banding, in which there appear sharp breaks of tone in areas which ought to shade seamlessly. We saw an example of this earlier, on page 51. With tonal shading across a wide area, such as with a clear sky through a wide-angle lens, any hint of banding is almost impossible to remove.

But why should there be banding in the first place? With a good sensor and minimal alterations in the processing, there rarely is. However, sensors with a low bit-depth, as in cheaper cameras, can display this effect. And for any image, major processing changes, such as those to brightness or contrast, or by using one of the increasingly common local-contrast controls, runs this risk.

This is intimately related to bit-depth. A higher bit-depth, which for most of us means 16 bits rather than 8 bits, has more capacity to render a range of tones. 8-bit color, although perfectly acceptable for final delivery of an image, is accurate to only 1 part in 256 per pixel. 8 bits per channel means that there are just 256 levels with which to reproduce the tones. High-end cameras record in 12 bits or 14 bits per channel. 12-bit measures to an accuracy of 1 part in 4026, and so is much better. 14-bit measures to 1 part in 16,104, which is better still. Nevertheless, by the time the image reaches the memory card, having been through the camera's on-board processor, it will be 8-bit if you have chosen to shoot JPEG. If, sensibly, you shoot in Raw, these original 12 or 14 bits will have been converted to a 16-bit image for opening in, say, Photoshop's 16-bit mode. Provided that you do processing and post-production in 16 bits, the risk of banding is very much reduced. With an 8-bit image, on the other hand, as the example on pages 80-81 shows, after processing the histogram is quite likely to show a tooth-comb appearance, with thin spikes. This damage to the image may show up only at high magnification, but for high quality black-and-white prints, it is not acceptable. Because there is no color to distract in the image, artifacts like noise and banding are likely to receive even more attention from anyone inspecting the image closely.

**ISO 100**  **ISO 400**  **ISO 1600**

*Noise is most visible in medium-to-dark tones that are smooth and lacking in subject detail.*

**Whole image**

# NOISE, BIT DEPTH, & SHADING

## HIGH ISO NOISE

**High ISO original**
*A night-time shot, of a Christmas "cabalgata" in Spain, taken at the extremely high ISO of 25,600.*

**Crop**
*In close-up, the noise is expectedly disturbing in color, but less so in black and white when the chrominance component is removed. Looking at each individual channel, the noise is strongest in most images in the blue channel, least in green.*

**Black and white**

**Red channel**

**Green channel**

**Blue channel**

**Default noise reduction**

**Noise reduction 100**

**Noise reduction 50**

## Noise filtering
*Noise can be filtered out during processing, but at a price. Compare these three Photoshop versions, the first with default noise reduction (0% Luminance), the second at 50% Luminance reduction, and the third at 100% reduction. The more you reduce, the softer and more "plastic" the effect.*

# NOISE NINJA

## Load profile
*Using a specialist noise-reduction software, Noise Ninja. This automatically searches for and loads a previously calculated noise profile for the camera and ISO setting.*

**Noise filter**
*A movable square selection (bounded in green) gives a preview of the noise reduction.*

**Noise filter adjusted**
*Controls allow for adjustment of strength, smoothness, and contrast.*

**Noise removed**
*Finally, the chosen settings are applied overall.*

# NOISE, BIT DEPTH, & SHADING

## 8-BIT AND 16-BIT COMPARISON

Original

Detail

| BLACK AND WHITE | |
|---|---|
| REDS | 120% |
| YELLOWS | 105% |
| GREENS | 40% |
| CYANS | -150% |
| BLUES | -124% |
| MAGENTAS | 80% |

Conversion settings

**Pre-processing**
*To demonstrate the importance of using a high bit-depth for major adjustments, a detail of this image is first converted to black and white.*

Crop before curve

| SHADOWS/HIGHLIGHTS | |
| --- | --- |
| **SHADOWS** | |
| AMOUNT | 39% |
| TONAL WIDTH | 43% |
| RADIUS | 200px |
| **HIGHLIGHTS** | |
| AMOUNT | 44% |
| TONAL WIDTH | 57% |
| RADIUS | 30px |
| **ADJUSTMENTS** | |
| COLOR CORRECTION | +20 |
| MIDTONE CONTRAST | +30 |
| BLACK CLIP | 0.01% |
| WHITE CLIP | 0.01% |

**Curve**
*First, a typical contrast S-curve is applied.*

**Shadows/Highlights**
*Next, Shadows/Highlights adjustments are made to further enhance contrast (the settings are deliberately extreme for this example).*

**16-bit**
*When applied to a 16-bit image, the histogram remains intact through both changes.*

**8-bit**
*However, when exactly the same changes are made to an 8-bit image, tonal information is lost, as evidence the tooth-comb appearance of the histogram.*

**16-bit after curve**

**16-bit after Shadows/Highlights**

**8-bit after curve**

**8-bit after Shadows/Highlights**

# INFRARED

Used sensitively, it takes the tonal qualities in photography further from realism than any regular black-and-white process, and brings an exciting unpredictability that can be highly stimulating creatively. Infrared photography has in fact been around since 1910, but was held back as a creative medium by two things—one was that the choice of film emulsions, and so the "look," was extremely limited, and the other was the difficulty in planning an exposure. Digital infrared has changed both of these completely. Not only are there several ways of shooting in these longer wavelengths, each with its own visual characteristics, but the software processing allows huge range of control after the event. Moreover, the result is instantly viewable, as with any digital image, on the camera's LCD screen, making results more predictable.

**Monochrome infrared represents one of the most creatively useful technological breakthrough in photography.**

First, a look at the principle of infrared photography and how it worked with film. The sensitivity of the human eye ranges from about 450 nm to about 700 nm (from what we call violet to what we call red), and peaks at 550 nm, which is yellow-green. Neither silver-halide film nor, as we'll shortly see, sensors, capture the same range. Silver halides capture much more violet and blue than does the eye, but stop short of about 525 nm. Special color dyes need to be added to film to extend its sensitivity even to visible light, and more are needed to extend the range into the near infrared. Infrared films are thus sensitive to visible light *and* near infrared. To photograph in infrared only, the visible light component needs to be eliminated, and this calls for a visually opaque filter, typically a Wratten 89B or Hoya R72. This makes exposures long and means viewing and composing before fitting the filter over the lens. We could do the same with a digital camera, but infinitely better is to have the sensor doctored, as described below.

**Sensor conversion**
*Professional sensor conversion in progress at ACS, a British specialist company (www.advanced cameraservices.co.uk).*

**Wavelengths**
*Daylight extends well into the infrared, but human vision stops just short. Unfiltered digital sensors peak in the infrared (hence their suitability for this conversion), and an infrared cut filter limits the sensor response to infrared by blocking longer wavelengths of visible light.*

**Myakka River**
*An image of palm trees in Florida's Myakka River reserve, shot on Kodak's black-and-white infrared emulsion (now discontinued). The pale vegetation and contrasty sky are typical, as are the pronounced grain and soft halation effects.*

# INFRARED

The reason I'm stressing the creative value of infrared is that if you agree with the argument that black and white releases creative potential in an image by stepping away from the assumed realism of color, then infrared does this to an even greater degree. Certainly, there are some well-known hallmarks of infrared monochrome, such as white foliage against inky black skies, but it is not even necessary to invoke these extremes. Because surfaces and objects reflect infrared wavelengths in ways that are unfamiliar to our eyes, the tonal scale and balance to some degree unexpected and different throughout. This alone makes infrared a new visual world to explore.

At the shorter end of their range, infrared wavelengths begin at around the point where the human eye loses sensitivity, which is at about 700 nm. To put this in perspective, the eye's sensitivity ranges from around 400 nm to 700 nm, peaking near the middle in the yellow-green part of the spectrum. Thermal imaging is at very much longer wavelengths. It is because we are simply not familiar with what things look like at wavelengths longer than 700 nm, that infrared images have a strange appearance. That they can be imaged but not seen directly is because film's sensitivity extends beyond that of the human eye into infrared. The situation is similar in digital photography: a silicon chip is naturally sensitive across a range from around 400 nm up to about 1200 nm, peaking at around 1000 nm. Indeed, camera sensors are so good at picking up infrared emissions that, during manufacture, they are fitted with an IR Cut Filter (ICF) in front, also known as a hot mirror filter. Remove this, which is part of the process of converting a camera for infrared photography, and the infrared emissions come flooding in. The visible wavelengths of course continue to be recorded at full intensity, so that the second part of conversion is to fit a sharp-cut filter that restricts most, or even all, of the visible wavelengths. The most popular filter cuts at around 720 nm, which allows just enough visible light in addition to the infrared to enable color infrared photography. And while our interest here is black-and-white infrared, the mild color response can be used to advantage by later applying hue adjustment, as we'll see on the following pages. For a pure monochrome infrared response, a filter that cuts at about 839 nm is an alternative.

One more thing needs to be done to the camera, which is to re-set the focus. As the infrared wavelengths are longer than those of visible wavelengths, they focus at a different point. This turns out to be more varied and complex than you might think, as different lenses refract infrared differently, but the bottom line is that the adjustment that needs to be made is as if extending the lens a little forward, as if focusing closer. The amount is small, typically around a third of one percent, but the effect can be to lose acceptable sharpness at wide apertures. In the conversion process, the camera is re-programmed, but even so, as most people choose the 720 nm conversion, which combines infrared with some visible, it's a wise precaution to stop down, to at least $f8$ for safety.

In practice, what does this mean for shooting? In comparison with IR film photography, life becomes infinitely easier. You can see what you are doing, a result of sorts is available instantly on the LCD screen (and if the color is often way off, the exposure information is reassuringly accurate), and exposure settings are for the most part within the handheld range. For example, at ISO 100, you could expect on a sunny day shutter speeds in the order of 1/200 sec at $f8$. Also, in most situations, the dynamic range is well contained, meaning that clipping issues are fewer than usual.

# INFRARED COMPARISONS

Digital infrared has less noise than the equivalent IR film grain, and also less halation. Here in this view of a valley in Colombia's Sierra Nevada de Santa Marta, the pale green vegetation and atmosphere-cutting effects are both strongly evident.

In some circumstances, the infrared effects are much less obvious. Here, shot on two different cameras, a man in yellow overalls whitewashes a wall. There is higher reflectivity in the infrared images from his overalls and from his skin, but apart from that there is little to distinguish between the two.

**Normal**

**Infrared camera**

Now, even though here our sole interest is black-and-white infrared, the color settings can be important. While you can process as desaturated, if you have the ability to adjust the color balance and saturation, this gives you extra room to play with hue adjustment. In order to do this, however, we need to be able to neutralise any color cast. Because most of the recorded information is into the red and away from the blue, typical infrared files, as you shoot them, appear suffused with red and magenta and need major white balance adjustment. This is often more than most cameras allow, hence the importance of shooting raw. Even so, Photoshop's ACR, for example, has a left-hand limit of 2000 K for color temperature. One solution is to preset the white balance to a surface that responds strongly to infrared, such as grass. Another is to create an infrared profile, as shown here. This is my preference, as it saves time when shooting. Then, once you have a more-or-less neutralised image, any features that are stronger in, say, blue or yellow, can be manipulated in the usual way when doing a hue adjustment (see page 110).

There is always a degree of unpredictability when shooting in infrared, as the reflectivity of surfaces at this end of the spectrum can differ from the way they look, and this is part of infrared's charm. You can expect vegetation to appear very light, almost like snow, because the chlorophyll in the leaves fluoresces strongly in the near-infrared, around 700 nm. This effect is actually least in healthy mature leaves and strongest in young, growing ones and in dying leaves. Another effect is that clear skies record very dark, and there is very good penetration of atmospheric haze. Both of these are due to a reduction of scattering relative to visible light. Probably the most typical infrared shot of all is a green-leaved tree and grass against a clear blue sky, and while this is dramatic, it is also in danger of becoming something of a cliché. Human skin also changes its appearance, as these infrared wavelengths penetrate it to some distance, and the result is that skin appears lighter than in visible light. At the same time, what may not always be attractive in portraits is that the eyes tend to record dark, typically contrasting strongly with the pale skin.

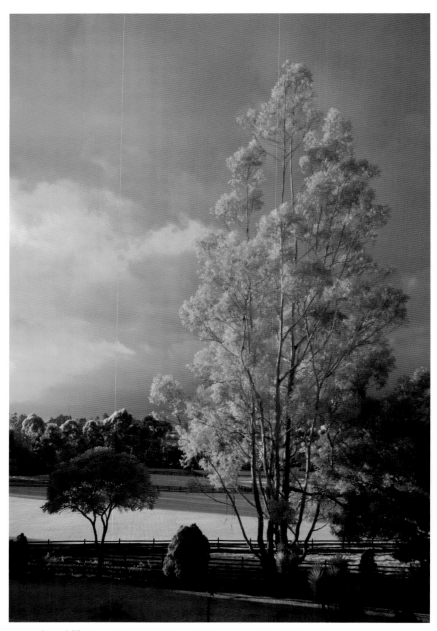

**Raw infrared file**

DIGITAL MONOCHROME

**Monochrome
interpretation 1**

**Monochrome
interpretation 2**

**Interpretations**
*The value of oversaturating a
color version of the raw file
during raw conversion is that it
lets you use black-and-white hue
adjustment to considerable effect.
Here, the color contrast between
sky and the eucalyptus leaves
allows several alternative
monochrome interpretations.*

## MAKING A PROFILE FOR INFRARED

One issue with an infrared conversion is the white balance, which after conversion typically falls below a raw converter's color temperature limit (for Photoshop's ACR and Lightroom, for example, this lower limit is 2000 K). Here is one way of bringing the white balance back into range, using Adobe's DNG Profile editor.

*1. First make a DNG file from the raw, using the raw converter, and then open it in DNG Profile Editor.*

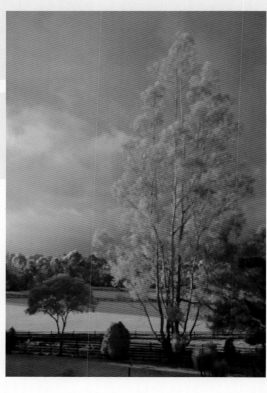

*2. Select the Color Matrices tab.*

*3. Lower the color temperature and adjust the tint with the White Balance calibration sliders. In this case, the temperature needed to be taken to the limit.*

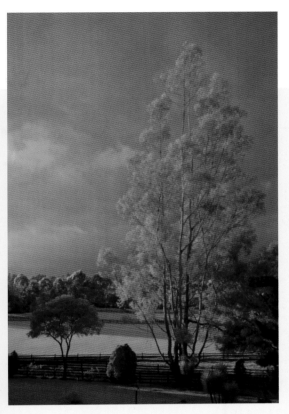

*4. Adjust the other hue and saturation sliders to taste (there is no realism with infrared, so it depends entirely on you). If the final result for infrared images will be in black and white, stressing color contrast at this stage will give you extra control later when making a black-and-white conversion from the processed TIFF.*

*5. Go to File > Save Recipe in order to save the work so that you can edit it later if necessary.*

*7. Back to Photoshop, open an infrared image in ACR and select the saved profile.*

| |
|---|
| ACR 4.4 |
| ACR 3.3 |
| ✓ Adobe Standard beta 2 |
| Camera D2X Mode 1 beta 2 |
| Camera D2X Mode 2 beta 2 |
| Camera D2X Mode 3 beta 2 |
| Camera Landscape beta 2 |
| Camera Neutral beta 2 |
| Camera Portrait beta 2 |
| Camera Standard beta 2 |
| Camera Vivid beta 2 |
| Nikon D200 IR_ex19095_02 |

*6. Go to File > Save Profile too.*

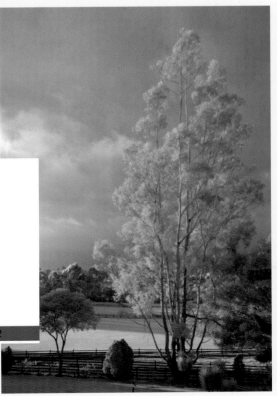

# YOUR PROCESSING WORKFLOW

In the new workflows, there is a trend towards concentrating as much of the processing as possible into the raw conversion, which offers you the additional choice of making the conversion at that stage or later, on a 16-bit TIFF. There is plenty of conflicting advice on the workflow sequence, but in reality, there are no truly compelling reasons for doing any particular procedure first, or last, or wherever. The purpose here is to present the basic procedures and show how you might consider sequencing them.

The underlying assumption here is that you are shooting raw, which gives the maximum opportunity for controlled processing. Not the least advantage is that there is some latitude to adjust the actual exposure. This is because of the extra dynamic range offered by the higher bit-depth of 12-bit and 14-bit capture in a good DSLR. The amount you can adjsut by depends on the sensor, the subject and the original exposure settings, and is hardly ever up to the theoretical maximum of two stops up or down, but you could normally expect a useful half to one stop range of adjustment. Note that this only applies to processing raw images, not to JPEGs or TIFFs, which have already been processed in-camera and reduced to 8-bits.

You can distinguish between processing procedures that always have to be considered for every image, and the special procedures that certain images might need to solve problems (such as over- or under-exposure in the first place, contrast, brightness, and so on). Processing workflow also varies according to the way you shoot, and indeed what you shoot. At one end of the scale are photographers, artists or enthusiasts, who are prepared to spend an infinite amount of time on one special image; at the other are those who will regularly process dozens at a time.

**There are now so many digital processing possibilities and decisions that it is becoming increasingly important to plan a logical workflow that suits the way you shoot.**

## ESSENTIAL AND OPTIONAL STEPS

Basic processing decisions that need to be considered for any image:

- Adjust exposure if raw, and if necessary set black and white points
- Decide contrast
- Set hue adjustment

Processing refinements either to taste or to help solve problems:

- Highlight recovery
- Shadow lightening
- Local contrast tonemapping
- Toning/split toning

# RAW CONVERSION OPTIONS

## Photoshop

*Photoshop's raw converter (ACR) offers a grayscale conversion that makes use of hue sliders. An alternative is to process in color at this stage, and convert later from the TIFF.*

## Lightroom

*Adobe LightRoom uses the same Raw converter as does Photoshop, but integrates it with all its other processing functions.*

## RAW CONVERSION OPTIONS CONTINUED

### Black and White Conversion

Filter Hue

0 ▲ 360  **60** °

Color Filter Strength

0 ▲ 100  **40** %

-100 ▲ 100  **0**

-100 ▲ 100  **0** %

### Aperture

*Aperture's Monochrome
Mixer offers a more
limited choice of hue
adjustment, restricting the
choice to percentages of
red, green, and blue.*

### Nikon NX

*Nikon's Capture NX performs its hue
adjustment by means of a hue selector
along a scale, then strength,
brightness, and contrast.*

▼ ☐ Color

Hue: ─────◉───── ‹ 0.0 ›

Saturation: ─────◉───── ‹ 0.0 ›

Luminance: ─────◉───── ‹ 0.0 ›

Range: ─────◉───── ‹ 1.00 ›

**CaptureOne**
*Capture One relies on preset profiles.*

**LightZone**
*LightZone, like Capture NX, uses a broad hue selector, but in the form of a color circle rather than a slider.*

**DxO**
*DxO Optics Pro, like Capture One, uses presets in its Color Modes window.*

# SILVER EFEX PRO

**T**his is a rare case where I will devote these two pages to a specific program (other than the ubiquitous Photoshop). As a plug-in, it works after the Raw processing, and there is no disadvantage to this if the image has been saved as a subtly graded 16-bit TIFF.

In addition to the usual controls offered by all processing software, including hue adjustment, Silver Efex Pro has its own selective method as an alternative to emulations of traditional dodging and burning. Under the proprietary name U Point Technology, which this software developer first introduced in Capture NX, the official Nikon processor, this works as follows. You add a Control Point by clicking on an object or area that you want to adjust. This automatically reads Red, Green, and Blue values and location. Size can be increased or decreased to change the reach of the particular Control Point, and the three standard adjustments offered are Brightness, Contrast (both self-explanatory) and what the manufacturer calls Structure. Structure is this software application's term for a kind of local contrast control. While this is now a fairly common procedure—adjusting contrast on a relatively small scale by taking into account the local neighborhood of pixels—the algorithms for selecting the area affected vary. Here, Nik Software has its own algorithm, which in the developer's words "increases/decreases the contrast inside an object without increasing the outside contrast (e.g. the structure of a tree but not the outline of the tree which could cause a halo effect)."

Also notable is film emulation, which is more comprehensive than most in that the choices offer not just grain structure, but tonal response also, accompanied by characteristic curves. These were shown on pages 62-67. For followers of the Zone System (pages 166-171), there is a useful 11-zone scale below the magnifying Loupe.

**All processing software offers black-and-white conversion, but one plug-in currently stands out for its devotion to mono and its powerful tools.**

## RECOMMENDED WORKFLOW

Before you can edit your image, you need to launch it in Photoshop, since it is a plug-in (a separately-bought extra tool which adds to the feature set rather than operating alone). From then on, the software manufacturer's recommended workflow for best results is as follows.

*1. See if one of the styles in the Style Browser is appropriate.*

## ZONE SYSTEM

A graduated scale with 11 zones, called the Zone System Map, covers the full tonal range of the image. Clicking on a zone or rolling the cursor over the Map causes that zone to be highlighted in the image, which helps identify areas of the same tonal value.

2. Adjust the overall image brightness, contrast, and structure.

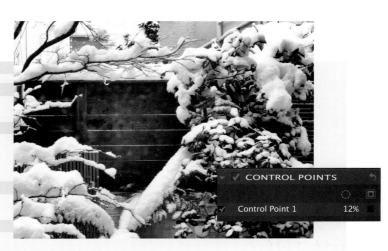

3. Make selective adjustments by adding control points to elements and areas in the image that may need it.

4. Choose a color filter for hue adjustment.

5. Choose a film type preset if desired.

6. Choose a stylization type if desired.

7. Review the image in the Loupe and apply the effects by clicking OK in Photoshop (or Save in Aperture).

# BASIC PROCESSING

**The increasing sophistication of raw converter software, with more and more controls and special algorithms being added, can easily obscure the basic principles.**

We can do more to bring out the best in the original capture than ever before, and that can only be good news, but faced with perhaps a dozen sliders, each of which will have an impact on the others, where do you begin? Moreover, while adjustments to exposure, black point and brightness, for example, are self-explanatory, the newer and more arcane inventions, such as highlight recovery, clarity and local contrast tonemapping are not at all transparent in what they do. Ultimately, the full solution is to spend more time learning what all the controls do and what effects you can see from them, but you can make a very effective start by thinking clearly about the priorities. There have always been a few basic principles in optimizing an image, back to the days of wet-processing and printing, and while the names of these may have changed, the core needs remain the same.

Reduced to the simplest, there are just three basic image qualities for a monochrome photography: brightness, contrast and tonal range. When you shoot, unless you exercise some kind of external control over the scene (such as lighting it, or using reflector), you can influence just the first of these, by choosing the exposure settings. Contrast and tonal range depend on the scene. When it comes to processing, however, each of these is adjustable. They are also interdependent. Moving one can affect another, so that even if you argue that one of the three takes priority, in practice you may still need to return to it after adjusting the others. Nevertheless, in an attempt to keep a clear view, here we'll look at each of these basic adjustments alone. Perhaps unexpectedly, we start with tonal range rather than brightness, because brightness can be altered in two ways—one takes the original capture data (the Exposure slider in Photoshop), the other works on processed data (the Brightness slider). Note also that contrast is a term that has been, and continues

to be, used in conflicting ways. In the days of film it was customary to use it to refer to the dynamic range as well.

## TONAL RANGE

Standard processing usually attempts to fit the tonal range of the image to the full scale available. This means, in effect, that the very darkest tones in the image are a fraction short of pure black, and the very lightest tones a fraction short of pure white. This is absolutely not compulsory, as we'll come to in Chapter 3, where your creative choices are discussed, but the truth is that the majority of black-and-white photographs tend to look their best like this. The examples here show how and why.

The histogram is the key display, whether you are looking at it in a Raw converter (like ACR), or in Levels or in Curves with it superimposed. In the terminology of film and wet-printing, when the tonal scale of the image just fits the scale of the histogram, you will have a fully-scaled image. Now, if the scene you photograph just fits the range of the sensor, from dark to light, and if your exposure is spot on, then the tonal range should fit the histogram perfectly. If the scene is flatly it, meaning that the dynamic range is less than that of the camera sensor, then the image as you captured it will be under-scaled, and a candidate at least for expanding its range. In this situation, you have the greatest choice of all in processing: extra room at left and right on the histogram to choose where to put your black and white points. More common, however, is a scene with a higher range than the sensor can cope with, so that the shadow end or the highlight end of the tonal range—or both—are squashed up against the ends of the scale. As we saw on pages 74-75, the more serious problem is highlight clipping, which is why the safe exposure decision for most high-range subjects is to hold the highlights. Nevertheless, as the Raw example here shows, there is some extra exposure latitude that you can usually recover in the raw converter, as well as the useful highlight recovery algorithm.

# SETTING BLACK AND WHITE POINTS IN RAW CONVERSION

Make sure that the shadow and highlight clipping warnings are activated at the top of the histogram. Then do one of the following:

**1.** Drag the Exposure slider until you can just see highlight clipping (red), then move a fraction darker until this disappears. Then move the Blacks slider until just before blue clipping warnings appear.

**2.** Click Auto, which will attempt to set the range so that there is no significant clipping, then adjust if necessary as above.

**3.** If either of the above makes the overall appearance too dark, use the Recovery slider to reduce or remove highlight clipping. Or alternatively, in the second step in the process, use the Brightness slider to lighten the mid-tones without significantly affecting the black and white points (see box Exposure vs Brightness, page 101).

*Exposure lowered until the clipping warning just disappears.*

| CAMERA RAW: BASIC | |
|---|---|
| EXPOSURE | -0.35 |
| RECOVERY | 0 |
| FILL LIGHT | 0 |
| BLACKS | 5 |
| BRIGHTNESS | +50 |
| CONTRAST | +25 |

| CAMERA RAW: BASIC | |
|---|---|
| EXPOSURE | +0.15 |
| RECOVERY | 0 |
| FILL LIGHT | 0 |
| BLACKS | 5 |
| BRIGHTNESS | +50 |
| CONTRAST | +25 |

*Exposure raised until clipping warning just appears.*

| CAMERA RAW: BASIC | |
|---|---|
| EXPOSURE | -0.35 |
| RECOVERY | 0 |
| FILL LIGHT | 0 |
| BLACKS | 13 |
| BRIGHTNESS | +50 |
| CONTRAST | +25 |

*Blacks slider moved in until clipping warning just appears.*

# BASIC PROCESSING

## SETTING BLACK AND WHITE POINTS IN RAW CONVERSION

▶▶

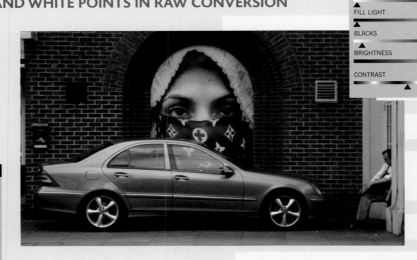

*Blacks slider lowered until clipping warning just disappears.*

| CAMERA RAW: BASIC | |
| --- | --- |
| EXPOSURE | -0.35 |
| RECOVERY | 0 |
| FILL LIGHT | 0 |
| BLACKS | 3 |
| BRIGHTNESS | +50 |
| CONTRAST | +25 |

| CAMERA RAW: BASIC | |
| --- | --- |
| EXPOSURE | -0.55 |
| RECOVERY | 0 |
| FILL LIGHT | 0 |
| BLACKS | 7 |
| BRIGHTNESS | +34 |
| | +47 |

| CAMERA RAW: BASIC | |
| --- | --- |
| EXPOSURE | -0.25 |
| RECOVERY | 0 |
| FILL LIGHT | 0 |
| BLACKS | 3 |
| BRIGHTNESS | +34 |
| CONTRAST | +47 |

*Click Auto. Still leaves some clipping in this case.*

| CAMERA RAW: BASIC | |
| --- | --- |
| EXPOSURE | -0.25 |
| RECOVERY | 0 |
| FILL LIGHT | 0 |
| BLACKS | 7 |
| BRIGHTNESS | +34 |
| CONTRAST | +47 |

*After Auto, adjust Recovery and Blacks to achieve no clipping.*

## SETTING BLACK AND WHITE POINTS IN AN ALREADY-PROCESSED TIFF

Do one of the following in Photoshop Levels:-

**1.** Drag the black-point Input slider on the left towards the right as far as the first group of pixels in the histogram. To check for accuracy, hold down the ⌥ key (Mac) or Alt key (Windows) as you do so. With the black-point slider the image will be pure white until you reach the first pixels—in other words, it will show at what point you clip the shadows. Now do the equivalent for the white-point slider on the right, dragging it towards the left. Hold down the ⌥ key (Mac) or Alt key (Windows) as you do so, and you will see white pixels appear out of black. The aim with each slider is to close in just up to the point of clipping.

**2.** Click the black-point dropper to activate it, then find the darkest shadow in the image and click on that. Find the darkest shadow using one of these methods:

  **a.** First dragging the black-point slider with ⌥/Alt key depressed as in step 1 (above).

  **b.** Going to Curves and using the eyedropper on the image, while seeing where each tone is located on the curve.

  **c.** Running any cursor across the image while seeing the results in the Info palette.

Do the equivalent with the white-point dropper.

**3.** Click Auto in the Levels dialog, or go to *Image > Adjustments > Auto Levels*.

*Here is the TIFF, not yet optimized, together with the histogram. Just a glance shows that there is room on the histogram scale at both ends to close up.*

24    1.00    255

*Drag in the left slider, holding down the ⌥/Alt key to display shadow clipping. Go in until you just see clipping, then pull out until there is just none.*

21    1.00    255

*The final black point setting.*

24    1.00    255

*Do the same at the highlight end, closing in until the clipping warning appears, then pulling back out.*

*The final settings and image.*

21    1.00    244

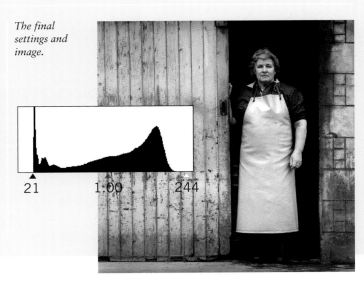

# BASIC PROCESSING

## DEFINITIONS

### Brightness
The most common word we use to describe the amount of light we see. Accurately, it is how we perceive luminance, which in turn is the amount of light that reaches the eye or sensor from a surface or a light source. Here, rather than get bogged down in the several ways of measuring light, the term brightness covers all of this. In digital photography, you can increase the brightness both in the exposure (allow more light to reach the sensor) and in post-production (by raising the values, mainly in the middle of the range).

### Contrast
Contrast is the ratio between high and low luminance values, but does not necessarily involve the entire tonal range. Quite commonly, it refers to the ratio excluding top highlights and lowest shadows.

### Tonal range
The ratio between the maximum and minimum values, from brightest to darkest. If the ratio is small, the photograph will look "flat." If a high ratio, it will look "contrasty." With a high ratio, the danger is clipping at either end, meaning losing information to solid white or solid black. For our purposes here, tonal range is equivalent to dynamic range.

## BRIGHTNESS
While there are real differences between luminance, luminous intensity, brightness and lightness, from the point of view of what looks satisfactory they are, frankly, academic. For appearance, which is what most photographers are concerned with, brightness is a perfectly adequate term. It is, indeed, not precisely measurable, because it is perceived luminance. That said, in raw conversion, a Brightness slider will raise vales within the black and white points, whereas the Exposure slider will affect clipping (see box Exposure versus Brightness, opposite).

With an already-processed image, altering brightness is a matter of dragging the values higher or lower, typically using a slider or by dragging a control point on a curve. There are several ways of doing this, depending on the processing software, but what they all have in common is that they affect the values within the tonal range, and leave the end-points alone. This is why traditional digital procedure is to set the black and white points first, then work on the overall brightness. The situation became rather more complicated with raw converters, because of the possibility to adjust the exposure itself. As explained above (pages 76-77), if your camera sensor captures in 12-bit or 14-bit, and your final destination is an 8-bit image, then potentially you have some exposure room for manoeuvre. In the same dialog window, however, you are also likely to have a brightness control (as in Photoshop's raw converter). Depending on the image, the differences in effect between the two may be minimal, so advice here varies as to which to use first.

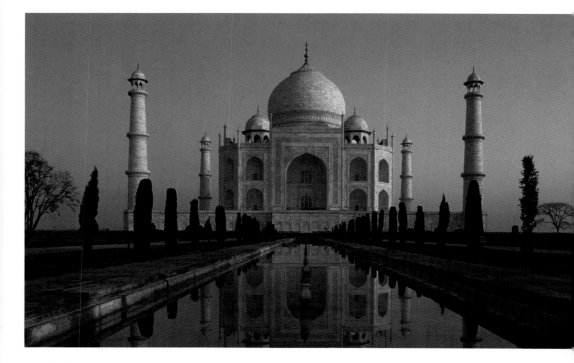

**Taj Mahal**
*The starting image.*

## EXPOSURE VERSUS BRIGHTNESS

In a Raw converter, altering the exposure is very close to changing the exposure settings at the time of shooting, and so will clip highlights if raised high enough (and shadow clipping also in the opposite direction). Nevertheless, Recovery and Fill sliders can pull back this clipping. The Brightness slider, on the other hand, works within the upper and lower limits, and so avoids, for the most part, clipping. The differences between adjustments using the two methods are usually very subtle indeed, almost to the point of there being no apparent difference. However, the Recovery slider, if used aggressively, will flatten some of the upper tones below the actual highlights.

**Lightening by using Exposure with Recovery**

**Lightening by using Brightness only**

**The starting point**

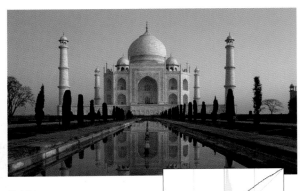

**Light tones**
*Lightening that favors the lighter tones.*

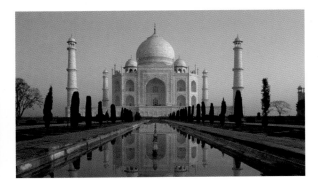

**Default**
*Lightening from the mid-point—the default.*

**Dark tones**
*Lightening that favors the darker tones.*

# BASIC PROCESSING

**Original image**

## CONTRAST

Contrast has become less easy to define since the invention of processing algorithms that work locally, meaning within a small neighborhood in the image. Also, it was regularly misused in the days of film to take in the total dynamic range. One thing that digital processing has forced is a more accurate way of thinking bout image qualities such as contrast. So, if you look at an image as a whole, its contrast is the ratio between the darkest tones and the brightest. But not necessarily the very darkest and brightest, however, as these may simply be outliers that sit apart, such as tiny specular highlights.

The traditional way of manipulating contrast is with a curve. Take one point in the upper part and drag it brighter, then a second point in the lower part and drag it in the opposite direction, and you have a classic S-curve and an increase in the overall contrast. The reverse—lowering the value of the brighter parts and raising those of the shadows—gives you a lower contrast.

However, contrast no longer needs to be applied globally, as this overall method is now called. You might, for example, have an image which is well separated spatially into two areas, darker and lighter, as in the example of a woman in a doorway here. What if you preferred to adjust the contrast of each of these differently? A straightforward manual way would be to make a selection of each area, and there are several ways of doing this, such as painting a mask, or loading a channel as a selection. You could then apply a contrast-enhancing S-curve to one area, and a contrast-reducing reverse S-curve to the other.

Simpler still is using one of the several local contrast tonemapping algorithms that work by searching around each pixel to look at its neighbors, and so do a similar thing, adjusting the contrast in a local area. Photoshop's Shadows/Highlights was one of the first of these (*Image > Adjustments > Shadows/Highlights...*).

**Step 1**
*In Photoshop, clicking on this small icon in the Channels palette automatically selects the lighter 50% of tones.*

*With this starting image, we want to heighten contrast slightly.*

DIGITAL MONOCHROME

102

**Step 2**
*Enhance this selection by increasing contrast.*

BRIGHTNESS/CONTRAST

BRIGHTNESS          20

CONTRAST           100

**Step 3**
*Lower the contrast in the lighter tones with a curve*

| Select | Filter | Analysis | 3D |
|---|---|---|---|
| All | | | ⌘A |
| Deselect | | | ⌘D |
| Reselect | | | ⇧⌘D |
| **Inverse** | | | ⇧⌘I |
| All Layers | | | ⌥⌘A |
| Deselect Layers | | | |
| Similar Layers | | | |
| Color Range | | | |
| Refine Edge… | | | ⌥ |
| Modify | | | |
| Grow | | | |
| Similar | | | |
| Transform Selection | | | |
| Edit in Quick Mask Mod | | | |
| Load Selection… | | | |
| Save Selection | | | |

**Step 4**
*Invert the selection to select the darker tones.*

**Step 5**
*Raise the contrast in these darker tones with a curve.*

SHADOWS/HIGHLIGHTS

**SHADOWS**

AMOUNT            15%

TONAL WIDTH       33%

RADIUS           200px

**HIGHLIGHTS**

AMOUNT            10%

TONAL WIDTH       20%

RADIUS            30px

**ADJUSTMENTS**

COLOR CORRECTION  +20

MIDTONE CONTRAST  +20

BLACK CLIP       0.01%
WHITE CLIP       0.01%

**Alternative**
*Instead of all the steps, use the Shadows/ Highlights adjustment to achieve a similar result.*

**Method 1**
*Apply a basic S-curve.*

**Method 2**
*Use the Contrast slider, which has essentially the same effect.*

BRIGHTNESS/CONTRAST

BRIGHTNESS          10

CONTRAST            80

**Method 3**
*For more control, this curve raises contrast only in the mid-grays, leaving the shadows and lighter tones as they were.*

# COLORS INTO TONES

**Y**ou want that red to be lighter, or that green darker? Well, you can have both at the same time if you want. Or any other color darker or lighter. This is the extent of post-processing possibility with digital shooting. The principle is not new—serious landscape photographers using film, for instance, have made use of colored filters for decades in order to darken skies, lighten vegetation and more. What is new, however, is the ability to be completely precise, and to do it in post-production so that you can see exactly what the effect will be on screen, without losing the color the original either.

**Possibly the greatest leap in creative potential that digital has brought to black and white is total control over how each individual color reproduces.**

Two things come into play here. One is the sensitivity of our eyes to different wavelengths—or colors, as we call them—and the other is the relative brightness of different hues. These two factors come together to create a scale of brightness-by-color that seems natural to us. We think of yellow as bright and purple as dark, by default. The human eye sees color because its cone receptors come in three varieties: red-sensitive, green-sensitive, and blue-sensitive (it is the absence of one of these that leads to color blindness). The chart on page 22 here shows which part of the spectrum each covers, and when added together, the total sensitivity peaks in the middle, which is yellow-green. The result is that we see colors as having different values. German poet and playwright J.W. von Goethe who attempted to put a measure to this, and suggested the following relative values: yellow 9, orange 8, red and green 6, blue 4, and violet 3.

In other words, shooting in black and white involves an expectation of how colors should reproduce as a plain tone. We expect a clear blue sky to be fairly dark, we expect Caucasian skin to look pale, green leaves and grass to look fairly light, and so on. None of this is precise, but we nevertheless sense when the tones appear not quite right. The blue-sensitive and orthochromatic films in the early days of photography characteristically produced images in which blue skies appeared white and Caucasian skin tones too dark. The development of panchromatic film (see page 16-17 and 22-23) was aimed at "correcting" just this unexpected result that the eye and mind intuitively found "wrong."

## COLOR PROPORTIONS

The proportions of primary and secondary colors that conforms to our normal perception, balancing stronger against weaker values.

**Orange / Blue**

**Orange / Green / Violet**

**Jia Nai Yun**
*The original color image, in which the only distinct color is the red of the pomegranate*

**Desaturated**
*Straight desaturation across the board, equal for all channels*

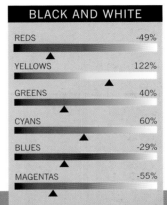

**BLACK AND WHITE**

| | |
|---|---|
| REDS | -49% |
| YELLOWS | 122% |
| GREENS | 40% |
| CYANS | 60% |
| BLUES | -29% |
| MAGENTAS | -55% |

**High red**
*Manipulating the sliders for the lightest rendering of the pomegranate.*

**BLACK AND WHITE**

| | |
|---|---|
| REDS | 198% |
| YELLOWS | 114% |
| GREENS | 40% |
| CYANS | -55% |
| BLUES | -105% |
| MAGENTAS | 19% |

**Low red**
*Manipulating the sliders for the darkest rendering of the pomegranate.*

**Red / Green**

**Yellow / Purple**

**Yellow / Red / Blue**

# LEARNING FROM FILM
# FILTERS

Channel mixing, which we come to in a few pages, follows a principle exploited for decades by photographers who used color filters. This was simply that a strongly colored filter passes its own color but absorbs its opposite, meaning complementary. For example, a strong blue filter allows all blue light (such as from a clear sky) to pass through completely, but holds back

**Controlling the relative brightness of different colors as they convert to black and white pre-dates digital by a long way.**

yellow light. Intermediate colors are affected relatively, so that violet passes through quite well, and yellow-green only a little. The effect on a monochrome image can be striking; using this example, a blue sky shot through a blue filter would be more or less white, but a lemon would be very dark (see the example "Blue filter effect" opposite).

The color circle, of which there are actually many versions but which was first created by Isaac Newton,

demonstrates better than anything the position of complementary, or opposing colors. With black-and-white film, selecting the appropriate filter allowed fine control of the resulting image, though it was not possible to preview the results.

Kodak's Wratten series, still made under license by Tiffen, was created as a standardized system of optical filters. There are, in fact, several different series under the overall Wratten umbrella, including Color Compensation, Color Conversion, and Light Balancing filters, but the series that concerns black-and-white photography is the Basic Color set. The filters that have long been considered generally useful for black-and-white photography are listed in the table here. In terms of precision, there are two kinds. The more common, known variously as long-pass or broad-cut, are for general use, while bandwidth or narrow-cut filters have more exact limits to the wavelengths they pass or absorb.

| WRATTEN NO. | COLOR | USE |
|---|---|---|
| 2A | Pale yellow | Absorbs ultraviolet radiation |
| 3 | Light yellow | Absorbs excessive blue, makes skies appear slightly darker |
| 8 | Yellow | Darkens blue sky towards the expected response of the eye |
| 9 | Deep yellow | Similar to 8, but a little more dramatic effect |
| 11 | Yellowish green | Darkens blue sky and slightly lightens definite green foliage |
| 12 | Deep yellow/Minus-blue | A definite darkening of blue skies and haze penetration |
| 15 | Deep yellow | More dramatic darkening of skies in landscape photography |
| 16 | Yellow-orange | Greater over-correction of blue than the yellow filters. Darkens green vegetation slightly. |
| 21 | Orange | Absorbs blue and blue-greens for higher contrast in many landscape situations |
| 25 | Red tricolor | Extreme darkening of blue sky and shadows under a blue sky, with contrast-heightening effect |
| 29 | Deep red | The strongest darkening of skies possible with a lens filter |
| 32 | Magenta/ Minus-green | The strongest darkening of greens |
| 34A | Violet | Darkens greens |
| 38A | Blue | Absorbs red, some ultraviolet and some green light |
| 47 | Blue tricolor | Lightens blue skies, enhances distance effects and often lowers contrast in landscape photography |
| 44A | Minus-red | Precise darkening of reds |
| 47B | Deep blue tricolor | Similar to 47, but stronger effect |
| 58 | Green tricolor | Darkens flesh tones for a more natural effect with Caucasian skin, and makes lips appear more definite |
| 61 | Deep green tricolor | Similar to 58, but stronger effect |

DIGITAL MONOCHROME

# FILTER EFFECTS

Original

Desaturated

Red filter effect

Blue filter effect

Green filter effect

Yellow filter effect

# DEFAULT CONVERSIONS

**W**hat is important to realize is that every one of these involves a decision as to how to do it. There is no such thing as a standard, "correct" method. Even the seemingly most innocuous and decision-free, which is desaturating each channel, tacitly assumes that treating each channel equally is somehow even-handed. Now that channel mixing is widely available, and we will come to that on the following pages, it should be clear to everyone that there is an open choice of how bright or dark different colors will translate to monochrome. With this in mind, the best ways to use your software's default conversion are as a quick preview and/or as a reference point against which to start channel mixing.

**Every digital image processing software offers a simple, no-thought, single-click method of turning a color image into monochrome. Some offer more than one.**

Here, for comparison, are a variety of defaults offered by different processing software. Note also that some offer presets with a bias towards certain effects, such as lighter, darker, higher contrast.

**Aperture**

**Capture One**

DxO Colormode

Lightzone

Adobe Camera Raw Auto

Lightroom grayscale

Capture NX

Adobe Camera Raw Default

109

# HUE ADJUSTMENT

**A**lthough the Channel Mixer persisted into Photoshop CS3, it was made largely redundant by the Black and White dialog, which expanded the number of channels available for adjustment to include cyan, yellow, and magenta. Also, for anyone shooting Raw, this hue adjustment was available within the Raw converter. Now, by the time of CS4, hue adjustment can be made for 8 hues, either in the Raw converter or later, in post-production. The color spectrum is divided into Reds, Oranges, Yellows, Greens, Aquas, Blues, Purples, and Magentas, which should be enough to satisfy the most obsessive monochrome photographer.

**Things have come a long way since the Photoshop introduction of the Channel Mixer, which was basically a one-stop dialog window for adjusting the relative strengths of grayscale conversion for each of the three channels, red, green, and blue.**

In truth, there are several ways of adjusting hues while converting to grayscale. Some pre-date the simple all-in-one Photoshop method, and involve copying channels into layers, then blending those. Using layer masks and adjustment layers increases the options, and also the complications. There are a few examples here of do-it-yourself hue adjustment and channel mixing to give you a sense of the range of techniques but, frankly, if you are working within Photoshop, its 8-hue slider approach is all most people could ask for. Other processing software offers similar choices, though packaged in a different way. Lightroom, naturally, borrows the Photoshop method, as it uses the same Raw conversion engine.

DIGITAL MONOCHROME

## COLOR WHEEL COMPARISONS

**Color original**
*The color original of Spanish Colonial cathedral, with two color wheels: the upper one a 12-section artists' perceptual, the lower one spectral 0°–360°.*

110

**Black and white**
*Photoshop's Black and White default settings.*

**Blue**
*Blue Filter preset.*

**Yellow**
*Yellow Filter preset.*

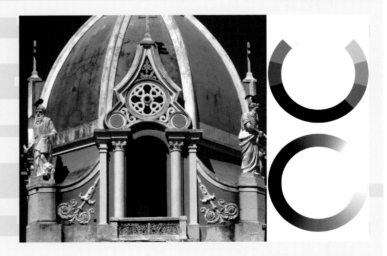

**Green**
*Green Filter preset.*

HUE ADJUSTMENT

# REVERSALS OF BRIGHTNESS

**As a demonstration of how powerful hue adjustment can be, if you have an image with definite and contrasting colors, it's possible to prepare two completely different, opposite interpretations of tone.**

Usually, the aim of hue adjustment is to produce a monochrome version that more-or-less equates with what we expect from the original color image. But this is not a rule, and one of the reasons for entering the world of monochrome in the first place is to have more than the usual freedom of expression.

Obviously, when the original colors are strong and pure, they react the most to hue adjustment, so for this example we'll take a striking contrast—a freshly painted parisian letterbox, and in strong, clear sunlight. Now, going back a few pages, we have a natural order of brightness for the colors we see, and yellow comes right at the top. For the human eye and brain, yellow is always bright, never dark (darken it and it becomes a different color to our senses: ochre). So the natural expectations for converting this image would be a bright yellow and a medium-dark blue.

What happens with a neutral, unadjusted conversion? Two things. A disappointing lack of contrast, nothing like that experienced in the color image, and the yellow darker than we would expect. If you came across the monochrome version with no reference to the color original, few people would imagine that the main color had been yellow. Before moving on to a high-contrast version, let's prepare by finding the settings that will come as close as possible to making the yellow and the blue equal in tone. As these colors are quite pure, and as the hue adjustment sliders are sharp-cut, it turns out that adjusting the blue alone does the trick.

Now for a conversion that maximizes the difference, with yellow as bright as possible. With this simple image, we need only the yellow and blue sliders, and neither affects the other. First, we raise the yellow tone. A level of 100 is as bright as we can get without clipping highlights, but this is a good perceptual match for a strong yellow. Second, we take the blue down. How much is a matter of taste. Note that the arrow and lettering have more cyan in them, and so they remain readable.

Next, the reverse. Interestingly, we don't need to lower the yellow slider very much before the tone goes distinctly dark, and the level chosen here, 19, is enough to throw the shadows very low. Raising the blue is next, but in order to retain some legibility in the lettering, the cyan slider also needs to be adjusted. Juggling the blue and cyan sliders together took a few tries.

**Paris postbox**
*The color original.*

# BLACK AND WHITE TOOL VARIATIONS

**BLACK AND WHITE**

| | |
|---|---|
| REDS | 50% |
| YELLOWS | 50% |
| GREENS | 50% |
| CYANS | 50% |
| BLUES | 50% |
| MAGENTAS | 50% |

**Neutral conversion**

*A neutral conversion, the equivalent of desaturation, has all the sliders at their mid-point.*

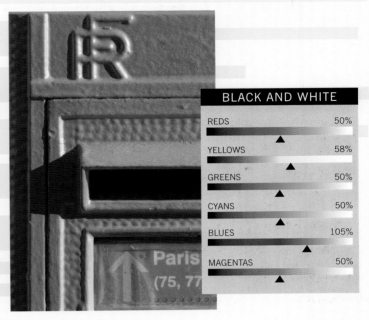

**BLACK AND WHITE**

| | |
|---|---|
| REDS | 50% |
| YELLOWS | 58% |
| GREENS | 50% |
| CYANS | 50% |
| BLUES | 105% |
| MAGENTAS | 50% |

**Equal tone**

*Adjustments to get as close as possible to matching the two tones.*

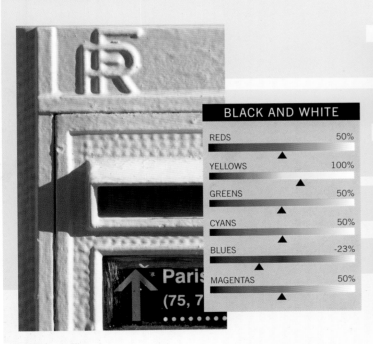

**BLACK AND WHITE**

| | |
|---|---|
| REDS | 50% |
| YELLOWS | 100% |
| GREENS | 50% |
| CYANS | 50% |
| BLUES | -23% |
| MAGENTAS | 50% |

**Maximum yellow**

*The maximum reasonable contrast with yellow bright.*

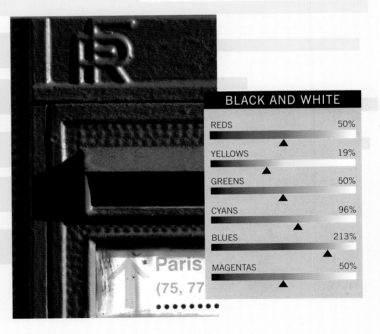

**BLACK AND WHITE**

| | |
|---|---|
| REDS | 50% |
| YELLOWS | 19% |
| GREENS | 50% |
| CYANS | 96% |
| BLUES | 213% |
| MAGENTAS | 50% |

**Minimum yellow**

*The maximum reasonable reverse contrast.*

# USING HUE TO CONTROL CONTRAST

A subtler and more satisfying method is to take advantage of the contrast of color within the original scene. If there are two important colors in an image that are in opposition, such as red and green, or blue and yellow, then adjusting the hues in the conversion to monochrome will easily do the trick. Raise or lower the tonal value of one color, and its opposing color will naturally go in the opposite direction.

**The traditional way to adjust contrast in an image is to drag the lighter values one way and the darker values in the opposite direction.**

There are some obvious but very specific examples, such as an orange photographed against a blue sky, or a tomato resting on green lettuce. These depend on the precise scene, and the example here shows what can be done. Taking careful decisions in the hue adjustment can make it unnecessary to deal with contrast later in the traditional way. Even more to the point, this technique

becomes particularly useful in outdoor photography in situations where there is a color contrats in natural lighting. The classic case is clear weather and bright sunlight. Without haze to soften the effects, anything exposed to direct midday sunlight will be lit by "white" light (around 5000-5500 K), but anything in shadow will be lit by a much bluer light coming from the sky, at anything from, say, 7000 to 10000 K). Now, the sky and shadows will respond precisely and obviously to either the blue slider or its opposite, which is a combination of red and yellow. Increasing red and yellow, and/or decreasing blue, will not just darken sky and shadow but also raise the overall contrast, seemingly changing the weather. Do the opposite and you will reduce the contrast. The maximum conditions for this are a clear atmosphere, high altitude, and a low sun (which has a lower color temperature and so redder light). The minimum conditions are haze and overcast.

**Juening Tulou**
*Color original. The mild contrast of cool, bluish hues and warm, orange ones can be exploited to enhance the contrast in the black-and-white conversion.*

# VARIATIONS

| BLACK AND WHITE | |
|---|---|
| REDS | 50% |
| YELLOWS | 19% |
| GREENS | 50% |
| CYANS | 96% |
| BLUES | 213% |
| MAGENTAS | 50% |

**Desaturation**
*A straight destauration reproduces the original contrast quite faithfully.*

**High contrast blue**
*One of the Photoshop Black-and-White conversion presets is High Contrast Blue, which raises the values of the cooler hues and lowers the warmer ones.*

| BLACK AND WHITE | |
|---|---|
| PRESET: High Contrast Blue Filter | |
| REDS | -50% |
| YELLOWS | -50% |
| GREENS | -50% |
| CYANS | 150% |
| BLUES | 150% |
| MAGENTAS | 150% |

| BLACK AND WHITE | |
|---|---|
| PRESET: High Contrast Red Filter | |
| REDS | 120% |
| YELLOWS | 120% |
| GREENS | -10% |
| CYANS | -50% |
| BLUES | -50% |
| MAGENTAS | 120% |

**High contrast red**
*Also increasing the contrast, though not by quite as much is the preset High Contrast Red, which raises the warmer hues and lowers the cooler ones.*

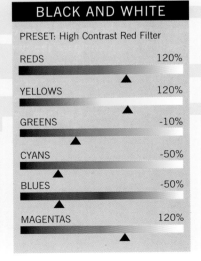

# USING HUE FOR DEPTH & ATMOSPHERE

**One of the most valuable hue controls in black-and-white photography is altering the sense of depth in a landscape shot. The technique, as old as panchromatic film, relies on passing or blocking blue, which increases with depth of atmosphere.**

The reason the blue hue is blocked is the selective scattering of light by the atmosphere; as the bluer wavelengths are shorter, they get scattered more easily by particles in the atmosphere, and so are more visible.

There are two ways to go: compressing aerial perspective by darkening the blues and so clarifying distant parts of the scene, and expanding it by lightening the blues to give a greater sense of depth. The traditional filter way was to use a red filter for the first (or orange or even yellow for a milder effect), and a blue filter for the second (see above, pages 104-105). The digital version follows exactly the same principle, but offers more control and, more importantly still, the chance to decide which route to take later, during processing.

Given choice, most people seem to have a natural reaction towards heightening contrast, probably because it has the effect of making images appear clearer, even sharper. Of course, this can be valuable and effective when converting to black and white, but it would be a mistake to treat it as a default. Going in the opposite direction, expanding the aerial perspective, can also expand the sense of scale in a landscape, and is generally a more delicate result. We can compare the two alternatives in two different landscapes here.

The first, on these two pages, is a sunrise view over the ancient city and ruins of Pagan in central Burma—actually taken from a balloon. I've chosen this because of the distinct blue that suffuses the atmosphere and includes wraiths of morning mist hanging between the trees. This, coupled with the reddish brickwork and gold leaf of the temples, is a color contrast that will certainly respond strongly to hue adjustment. But a point to note is that most landscapes are not by nature super-saturated, and if they have a significant amount of vegetation, the colors can be complex. Greens in particular are very rarely a rich green, and can contain yellows and even reds. When doing this kind of atmosphere control, vegetation greens are often the joker in the pack, and need to be watched carefully. We'll see more on this in a few pages when we look mainly at vegetation.

The first version aims to remove any sense of mist and haze, and the starting point is the High Contrast Red preset in Photoshop's Black and White conversion tool. From this, the red slider is taken up even further until just before the lightest reddish hues would clip to pure white. The result is a quite spectacular clarification, with almost no trace of the morning mist left, and high visibility all the way to the distant hills. Whether it is successful or not, however, is open to question. The opposite direction aims to enhance mist and haze, so the blue slider is the first control to use. The limit for its final setting is the reaction of the sky in the upper middle of the frame—this needs to be held below clipped pure white. Next, the red and yellow sliders are adjusted downwards to increase the silhouette effect of the temple, particularly the largest, by darkening them. The tree-tops in the lower half of the frame are a little problematical, because they contain cyan and some blue. Plenty of control available, but the final settings were chosen to fade the tones of the trees from dark in the left foreground to mid-gray in the middle distance.

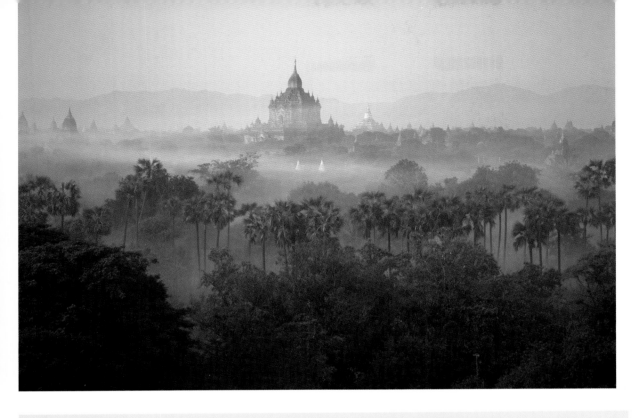

**Original**
*Color original, with early morning shade adding blue to the atmosphere and the mist.*

## VARIATIONS

**High contrast red**
*Photoshop's preset High Contrast Red, adjusted to further lighten the red response.*

| BLACK AND WHITE | |
|---|---|
| REDS | 187% |
| YELLOWS | 120% |
| GREENS | -10% |
| CYANS | -50% |
| BLUES | -68% |
| MAGENTAS | 120% |

| BLACK AND WHITE | |
|---|---|
| REDS | 16% |
| YELLOWS | 43% |
| GREENS | 73% |
| CYANS | 58% |
| BLUES | 127% |
| MAGENTAS | 90% |

**Blue plus**
*Custom settings to lighten the blue, while integrating the varying shades of green in the trees.*

# USING HUE FOR DEPTH & ATMOSPHERE

The second image is more conventionally low in color saturation, but covers a depth of a few miles (a mile is 1.6 kilometers) and has mountains in the distance that make a substantial part of the scene. In both versions, handling the whites of the clouds and snow was crucial, and the danger of clipping set limits to a number of the sliders. As a reference, I first made a default desaturation result, which already shows an expansion of aerial perspective.

For the compressed landscape version, blue and cyan were taken far down (the image is much less saturated than the previous example from Burma, and so the hue response more sluggish). Also, I decided it would be more effective if the tone of the grass was raised to match the distant hill-slope tones, so that there was no shading of tone from foreground to background. The effect has punch, although the hovering tern in the near-middle distance does not stand out particularly well.

Moving on to the opposite version, there is not a great deal to do to improve on the default desaturated result. Lowering the blue, however, removes the shading in the cliffs at left and lowers the contrast overall on the hills, thus flattening the distance. The blue sky is also a little paler. Finally, to enhance the foreground-to-background transition, I darkened the grass.

**Color original**

# BLACK AND WHITE VARIATIONS

**Desaturation**
*A straight desaturation made for reference.*

| BLACK AND WHITE | |
|---|---|
| REDS | 162% |
| YELLOWS | 153% |
| GREENS | 200% |
| CYANS | -118% |
| BLUES | -148% |
| MAGENTAS | 50% |

**Compress atmosphere**
*Depth compressed by lowering blue and cyan strongly, and raising red.*

| BLACK AND WHITE | |
|---|---|
| REDS | 107% |
| YELLOWS | 34% |
| GREENS | 77% |
| CYANS | 192% |
| BLUES | 120% |
| MAGENTAS | 80% |

**Expands atmosphere**
*Depth expanded by raising blue and cyan.*

# USING HUE FOR VEGETATION

**Hue adjustment to control the tones of vegetation is not as straightforward as dealing with skies and depth in landscapes.**

One reason it's so difficult to balance hue adjustment when shooting plant life is that vegetation greens are usually anything but saturated, and include yellows and sometimes reds. Another is that a variety of vegetation—different species of tree, for example—can involve different hues and different overall tones. Usually, an amount of juggling and trial-and-error is involved. To focus on the niceties of green hues and tones, I've chosen a single picture to work on. This is a view of one of the famous gardens in Suzhou, China, called Zhuozheng Yuan. In keeping with Chinese gardening tradition, color is sparse, and here resides just in the pale yellow-greens of weeping willows. The distant pagoda is an important part of the design, and incidentally an example of "borrowed landscape."

As a first step, let's see what a default desaturation looks like. Not at all successful; the trees are darker than the eye expects them to be, and show none of the separation from the rest of the scene that they do in color. What we should aim for is a lighter rendering, keeping contrast with the other elements in the picture. The first version uses the green slider alone to lighten the foliage, while moderate reductions to red, cyan and blue darken the pagoda in the distance. This is only moderately successful, as he foliage and pagoda are too similar in tone.

Let's see how far we can lighten the greens. This particular green carries a high proportion of yellow, so by concentrating on the yellow slider to achieve the lightening, we not only get a lighter result overall on the foliage, but we also now have a valuable contrast of shading within the greens. To accentuate the contrast with the pagoda, cyan and blue are taken to their minimum. Compare this with Photoshop's Infrared preset. This too relies on lightening the greens and yellows (to mimic the response of chlorophyll to infra red), but is more exaggerated.

Finally, having seen that varying the yellow and green sliders can increase contrast within the foliage, let's see how far this "internal" contrast can be taken. Striking, certainly, but a little odd. All in all, the second version seems to be the most successful.

**The color original**
*In the original the green weeping willows stand out clearly, while the other leaves have more mixed tones.*

# VARIATIONS

### Default
*The desaturated result has the leaves too dark, and the trees merge with everything else.*

### Raise greens
*In this version, the green slider is raised, while red, blue, and cyan are lowered.*

| BLACK AND WHITE | |
| --- | ---: |
| REDS | -44% |
| YELLOWS | 53% |
| GREENS | 235% |
| CYANS | -38% |
| BLUES | -35% |
| MAGENTAS | 80% |

### Lighter
*For a lighter rendering, use is made of the yellow slider, with blue and cyan taken to their minimum.*

| BLACK AND WHITE | |
| --- | ---: |
| REDS | -81% |
| YELLOWS | 207% |
| GREENS | -57% |
| CYANS | -101% |
| BLUES | -100% |
| MAGENTAS | 80% |

### Simulated infrared
*Photoshop's preset "Infrared" conversion.*

| BLACK AND WHITE | |
| --- | ---: |
| REDS | -40% |
| YELLOWS | 235% |
| GREENS | 144% |
| CYANS | -68% |
| BLUES | -3% |
| MAGENTAS | -107% |

| BLACK AND WHITE | |
| --- | ---: |
| REDS | 276% |
| YELLOWS | 144% |
| GREENS | -139% |
| CYANS | 101% |
| BLUES | 142% |
| MAGENTAS | 50% |

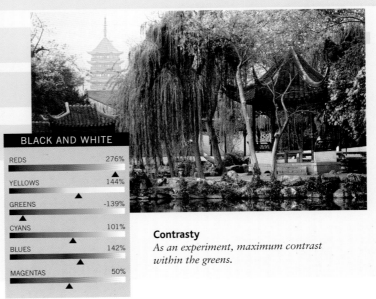

### Contrasty
*As an experiment, maximum contrast within the greens.*

# SKIN TONES

When most people refer to skin tones, they mean the shades of color. Here we're being literal—the actual tonal value, the brightness of skin when the image is converted to monochrome. Skin colors are among the strongest "memory colors," meaning that we are so familiar with and sensitive to the way they should appear that the "correct" appearance in a photograph is embedded in our memory. Even without necessarily being able to identify in which way the balance is skewed, most of us can immediately sense whether or not skin color in an image looks right or not. The same thing happens with a black-and-white image. If we know the person, or at lest have an idea of where they come from, we have a feeling for the "right" tonal value.

This, of course, varies greatly with ethnic group, and is not simply to do with darker versus lighter, but also involves the general color cast. As distinct examples, think of what we call rosy cheeks, or an olive complexion. Color complicates the conversion to monochrome, because of the huge choice in hue adjustment. Here, it will pay to take a more analytical approach to the image, and before making the conversion from an already processed TIFF, I want to measure the individual colors and the average brightness. Let's take three contrasting examples of skin: one blonde, pale Caucasian, another brown, the third black. The original three images were processed with very little alteration to the overall exposure and brightness. To all intents and purposes they are as shot, meaning that they closely resemble the original impression (confirmed by the camera's LCD preview at the time). This is important for this exercise, as we need to take these originals as a reliable starting point. Also important is that I chose all three for being taken under cloudy diffused light, which has a reliable color temperature.

> **When most people refer to skin tones, they mean the shades of color. Here we're being literal—the actual tonal value, the brightness of skin when the image is converted to monochrome.**

**Different tones**
*In a world with a wealth of different skin tones, it is important to know how to handle each one.*

## CAUCASIAN SKIN.

This is very much at the pale end of the scale. The red square is the sample area, taken in Photoshop using an 11 × 11 pixel average. We're taking the sample from the forehead, which has no shadows across it. The Info palette has been set to show RGB readings in the first column and HSB in the second, and from the latter we can see that the overall brightness is high at 92%. Also, while you would expect a white skin to have an overall pinkish cast, this has only a very mild bias. The conversion is neutral, using desaturation rather than a mix of hue sliders. The result is as most people would expect, and the conversion uncomplicated. However, as an experiment, see what visual difference there is from just a small change of overall brightness. Here, I've selected just the face by painting a mask over it to make a selection. What is interesting is that just the small reduction of 15% gives the impression of a slight tan, while the same small increase verges on high key. But ultimately, the "right" value is a matter of taste.

**Caucasian skin**
*Default conversion using desaturation.*

**Caucasian skin**
*Very pale Caucasian skin shows just a hint of pink. The bar on the right is the same color and brightness as the sample area in the red box.*

Caucasian skin color to black and white

| Color | Desat | -15 | +15 |
|-------|-------|-----|-----|
| R: 234 | | | |
| G: 218 | | | |
| B: 220 | | | |

**Desaturated -15**
*The face only—not the background—has been darkened very slightly, by 15%.*

**Desaturated +15**
*The face only, has been lightened by 15%.*

SKIN TONES

# SKIN TONES

### BROWN SKIN

The girl here is from Eritrea. Disregarding the leaf she has stuck on her forehead (it is reputed to have healing properties), we take the sample from close by. This is directly comparable with the Caucasian-skin sample, but what a difference. The brightness is below average at 44% (though it would be higher from the cheeks), and red figures strongly. Note also the low blue value

Brown skin color to black and white

| Color | Desat | -15 | +15 |
|-------|-------|-----|-----|
| R: 57 | | | |
| G: 45 | | | |
| B: 33 | | | |

which helps desaturate the overall color to brown. The monochrome conversion is again a straight desaturation, and I've supplied the same variations as above—up 15% and down 15%. Here, in contrast to the Caucasian skin, there seems to be more acceptable latitude, because this mid-to-dark toned skin is not close to either brightness limit—there are no obvious benchmarks of tone against which to judge it. Now we could take a different approach to adjusting the brightness by manipulating the hue sliders, but for the purposes of comparison with the other two skin types, we'll leave that particular exercise to the example of the two windswept male faces. Interpretation of tonal value with pale skin than with dark.

**Medium-to-dark brown skin**

**Default desaturation**
*Default conversion using desaturation.*

**-15**
*The face only, darkened by 15%.*

**+15**
*The face only, lightened by 15%.*

### BLACK AFRICAN SKIN.

Here, there are actually huge difference in tone betwéen ethnic groups, especially in southern Sudan where this photograph was taken. The ethnic group in this case is Dinka, whose skin is at the dark end of the scale. Now one of the things that happens visually with pronounced black skin is that it reflects more than do lighter shades, and the result is

Black African skin color to black and white

| Color R: 88, G: 75, B: 74 | | | |
|---|---|---|---|
| Color R: 57, G: 45, B: 33 | | | |
| | Desat | -15 | +15 |

**Dark skin**
*Showing highlight reflections.*

**Default desaturation**
*Default conversion using desaturation.*

# USING HUE ADJUSTMENT FOR DIFFERENT EFFECTS

These two faces are Caucasian, but windswept (the two men are archaeologists, so out in the open air a great deal). These condition gives a strong red component, and we can use it to make quite subtle changes to the monochrome tone. With a straight desaturation for comparison (with the reddish areas of the faces typically a little too dark in monochrome), there are two other versions, one raising the red channel, the other raising the yellow channel for lightening. While both have the same approximate effect, note that raising the red channel reduces the contrast across the faces in comparison to using the yellow channel. This can be useful for fine-tuning shading.

**BLACK AND WHITE**

| | |
|---|---|
| REDS | 75% |
| YELLOWS | 50% |
| GREENS | 50% |
| CYANS | 50% |
| BLUES | 50% |
| MAGENTAS | 50% |

**Default**
*Default conversion using desaturation.*

**Red raised**
*Raising the red channel to lighten the skin.*

**Yellow up**
*Raising the yellow channel to lighten the skin.*

**Original**
*Two faces with a relatively strong red component.*

**BLACK AND WHITE**

| | |
|---|---|
| REDS | 50% |
| YELLOWS | 75% |
| GREENS | 50% |
| CYANS | 50% |
| BLUES | 50% |
| MAGENTAS | 50% |

-15                    +15

a higher contrast across the face. The forehead sample is somewhere in the middle of this range, and shows a brightness of 35%, but a second sample from a darker area on the cheek goes down to 22%. The full range goes from 60% at the tip of the nose to 10% in the under-chin area. The color is limited, actually with about the same difference between red, blue and green as the pale Caucasian skin, although slightly more saturated in the darker non-light-reflecting areas. The brightness variations are perceptually less different than the other two examples, and one of the lessons here is that there is less latitude in interpretation of tonal value with pale skin than with dark.

# SPECIFIC COLORS

**A different kind of approach is called for when there is one significant color in the scene.**

Its importance can be due to all kinds of reasons, including the nature of the subject, the fall of lighting across the scene, or the special qualities of an uncommon color. The image I've chosen here is of lavender fields in Provence, in the south of France, and this annual crop is clearly the main subject of the shot—at least in the color version—despite the old abbey in the grounds of which it grows.

The methodology for this kind of dominant-color image involves first deciding whether its importance as a color will even translate into monochrome, then deciding what sort of tonal relationship it should have with the other elements in the frame (the degree of contrast or similarity, and how eye-catching), and finally the methods of isolating and altering that particular hue. In this shot, the special nature of the lavender hue becomes meaningless in black and white, but that it is lavender the flower, growing in distinctive busy rows, remains just as significant. In other words, it still warrants being the center of attention, though for its form and what it is rather than its color. It still needs to be an eye-catching part of the picture. So, the next decision is how to make it stand out, and the obvious aim is by contrast with as many of the other elements as possible. We can reject making it darker, which would simply look weird.

The hue adjustments applied here are in several steps, but all with the aim of making the sunlit rows of lavender lighter than the surroundings (which includes the sky). This will draw maximum attention to them. The sky in particular will need to be dark, so as not to compete for the viewer's attention. As usual, my first step is to make a default conversion as a reference—a base against which to work. This default is the Photoshop version, slightly different from a straight desaturation. Fine as far as it goes, but not if we want to favor the lavender as much as possible.

First step is to isolate the lavender hue and lighten it. It is made up of blue, magenta and red. At the same time, however, we want to do this without affecting the sky, which is blue. Now, the sky contains some cyan and no magenta, so that lowering the former to its minimum, and raising the latter to its maximum should give maximum contrast between lavender and sky. And it does. Raising red enhances this contrast. There is green mixed in with the purple of the lavender, so my decision here is to make it as light as the rest of the crop. Raising green does this, while lowering yellow evens out the lightness within the greens.

**Color original**
*Lavender field in Provence.*

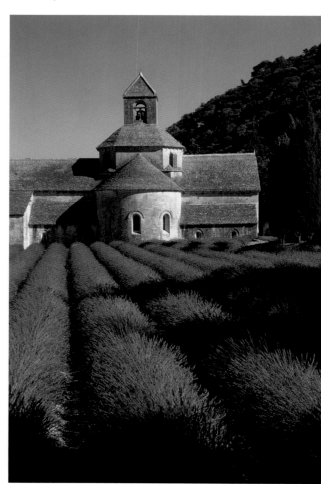

# DEFAULT AND MAXIMUM

**Default**
*Photoshop's
default conversion.*

### BLACK AND WHITE

| | |
|---|---|
| REDS | 40% |
| YELLOWS | 60% |
| GREENS | 40% |
| CYANS | 60% |
| BLUES | 20% |
| MAGENTAS | 80% |

### BLACK AND WHITE

| | |
|---|---|
| REDS | 136% |
| YELLOWS | -62% |
| GREENS | 185% |
| CYANS | -200% |
| BLUES | 43% |
| MAGENTAS | 300% |

**Maximum lavender**
*Adjustments to
maximise contrast
between a light
lavender and as much
else as possible darker.*

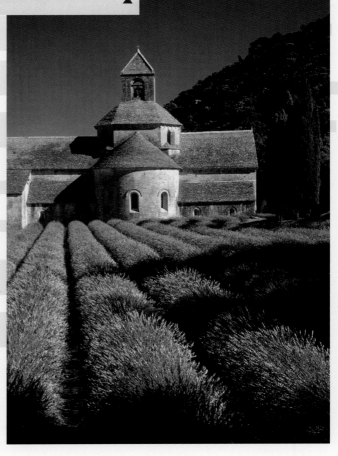

# HANDLING OPPOSITES

P rovided, of course, you want them to contrast with each other in the black-and-white version (lightening or darkening both together would involve merging two different versions of the image). By opposing colors I mean complementaries, as already shown on pages 102-103, and these do not have to be so strong and saturated as the swatches there in order to react well to the hue sliders during conversion.

**Potentially, controlling the tonal behavior of opposing colors is the easiest of all.**

The example here is relatively unsaturated, but still distinct in the color contrast between the yellowish cheroots in a Burmese street stall and the blue-painted shelves. The default conversion (Photoshop's default) in fact does a good job of maintaining the color contrast and giving an expected result. Nevertheless, let's see what can be done to enhance the contrast. Here, the key light tone chosen is the front end of the largest bundle of cheroots, which I want as bright as possible

without appearing white. This means striking the right balance between red and yellow when raising those sliders, as both are part of the cheroot color. As for the painted shelves, lowering the blue is the obvious approach, but note that the sunlight parts contain more cyan. Here, the cyan has been adjusted downwards to remove them—not necessarily a good thing for the picture, but done here to show that it can be done.

Now, one of the features of opposing colors in an image is that it is nearly always possible to make a reverse contrast conversion—the contrary, that is, of what the eye expects to see. We already saw this in action on pages 110-111. Here, in more subdues color circumstances, it is still a valid possibility. Certainly, it looks strange and unexpected if you already know what the original colors were, but to a viewer coming to the monochrome image alone, it works. Still, between these three versions the choice is down to taste.

**Color original**
*Blue Burmese
street stall*

**Default**
*Photoshop default conversion (the settings are the same as those on page 127).*

## RED AND BLUE EMPHASIS COMPARISON

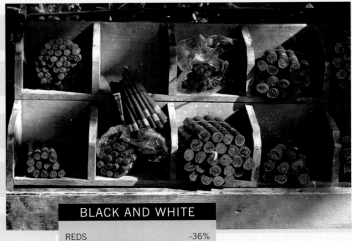

### BLACK AND WHITE

| | |
|---|---|
| REDS | 136% |
| YELLOWS | 90% |
| GREENS | 62% |
| CYANS | -12% |
| BLUES | 29% |
| MAGENTAS | 80% |

**High Red**
*Adjusted to exaggerate the color contrast, with the cheroots lighter.*

### BLACK AND WHITE

| | |
|---|---|
| REDS | -36% |
| YELLOWS | 30% |
| GREENS | 14% |
| CYANS | 254% |
| BLUES | 127% |
| MAGENTAS | 80% |

**High blue**
*The reverse adjustment, exaggerating the color contrast but with the cheroots darker.*

# HANDLING ADJACENTS

**When an image has groups of important colors that are similar to each other, and yet which you want to separate tonally in the monochrome version, hue adjustment can be at its most delicate and demanding.**

Changing one affects the others, so that there are always compromises to be made, and the procedure calls for some fine distinctions to be made between component colors. In other words, do not expect a quick fix with images similar to the examples here and on the following pages.

The first example is an exercise in handling the warm sector of the color circle—reds, oranges, and yellows. The image is of a table by designer Maarten Baas with two gilded cups, and while there is distinct red in the table and yellow in the gold cups, they both share orange. In fact, to some extent they share all three hues available as sliders. As this will be a delicate operation, let's take color samples in the same way that we did for skin tones. This confirms that the yellow slider will be important in raising the value of the gold.

For a change, as for the most part we have up to now been making conversions on already-processed TIFFs, here we will do the hue adjustment in Adobe Camera Raw—the Photoshop Raw converter. One good reason for this is that currently, Photoshop's ACR has an orange slider, which its Black and White converter does not. And we will need it.

To begin, the image is fairly accurately exposed and color balanced as shot, but we'll choose the standard Auto setting. Next, moving to the Grayscale window, we can take a judgment on the neutral default settings—as expected, but not enough tonal separation between cups and table. So, the next step is to darken the red of the table. Here, I'm cheating a little, because I can guess in advance that the orange slider will be needed to lighten all except the gold highlights (which are strongly yellow), so we can take the red down a little darker than we will eventually want.

The next step is to raise the highlights on the gold cups, using the yellow slider. This affects hardly anything else. Finally, for the hue adjustment, the orange is raised; this lightens everything slightly and, more important, reemphasizes the dappled reflections on the side of the table. As a last touch, once the image has been processed into a TIFF, the background is cleaned up by first, selecting it using the Quick Selection tool, then applying a lightening curve.

DIGITAL MONOCHROME

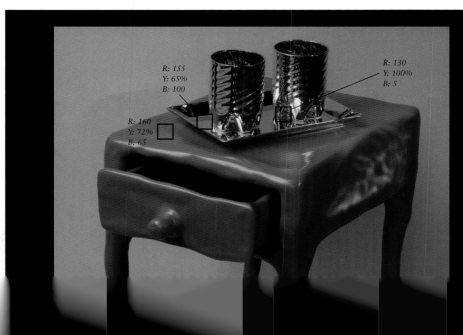

R: 155
Y: 65%
B: 100

R: 160
Y: 72%
B: 65

R: 130
Y: 100%
B: 5

**Original**
*The color image processed with default settings, and with three sample areas analyzed.*

**Final image**
*The final monochrome result after ACR.*

# RAW CONVERSION

**CAMERA RAW: BASIC**

| | |
|---|---|
| TEMPERATURE | 3700 |
| TINT | -7 |
| EXPOSURE | 0.00 |
| RECOVERY | 21 |
| FILL LIGHT | 0 |
| BLACKS | 2 |
| BRIGHTNESS | +55 |
| CONTRAST | +45 |

**Step 1**
*Auto color settings applied in Photoshop's ACR.*

**Step 2**
*In the Grayscale window, the default, neutral, settings.*

**HSL/GRAYSCALE**

| | |
|---|---|
| REDS | 0 |
| ORANGES | 0 |
| YELLOWS | 0 |
| GREENS | 0 |
| AQUAS | 0 |
| BLUES | 0 |
| PURPLES | 0 |
| MAGENTAS | 0 |

**HSL/GRAYSCALE**

| | |
|---|---|
| REDS | -30 |
| ORANGES | 0 |
| YELLOWS | 0 |
| GREENS | 0 |
| AQUAS | 0 |
| BLUES | 0 |
| PURPLES | 0 |
| MAGENTAS | 0 |

**Step 3**
*Using the red slider to darken the table.*

**Step 4**
*Raising the yellow slider to lighten the highlights on the gold cups.*

**HSL/GRAYSCALE**

| | |
|---|---|
| REDS | -30 |
| ORANGES | 0 |
| YELLOWS | +79 |
| GREENS | 0 |
| AQUAS | 0 |
| BLUES | 0 |
| PURPLES | 0 |
| MAGENTAS | 0 |

**HSL/GRAYSCALE**

| | |
|---|---|
| EDS | -30 |
| RANGES | +28 |
| ELLOWS | +79 |
| REENS | 0 |
| QUAS | 0 |
| LUES | 0 |
| URPLES | 0 |
| AGENTAS | 0 |

**Step 5**
*Raising the orange slider to lighten table and cups overall.*

**ACR output**
*The processed TIFF as handed over from ACR to Photoshop.*

**Step 6**
*Having made a selection of the background with the Quick Selection Tool (note the compressed histogram, which is of the background only), a lightening curve is applied.*

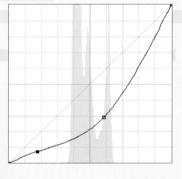

# HANDLING ADJACENTS

**T**he sky is an intense blue, but shades in brightness toward the horizon, and the water contains a mixture of desaturated colors. The water, nevertheless, is one element that we might want to adjust for contrast. As with the previous image, we can start by analyzing the key colors. For this, in Photoshop, the Info palette is useful, particularly if we open a second measurement in CMYK. This gives us a cyan measurement, even though the units are different from the RGB (percentage instead of levels from 0 to 255). Two sky samples show that cyan is relatively higher in the paler regions (even though there is absolutely more, 95% to 70%) in the stronger, higher regions. There is also a strong cyan presence in the higher reflections of the sky in the river, meaning that the cyan slider will also affect these. And there is a strong presence of green in the water.

Blues and cyans both work to lighten the sky, but favoring the blue over the cyan evens out the sky overall, which here can be useful. See also the effect of the cyan on the reflections higher up in the water. The lower part of the river, closer to the bottom of the frame, contains green, and raising the green slider to the maximum lightens the river more, which relates to the light treatment of the sky. Or, an alternative is to darken the green for a stronger contrast with the sandbanks—also valid.

**For the next example of an image with similar but important colors, and a need to separate. I've chosen this panorama of the First Bend of the Yangtse River.**

**Measurements**
*Samples of blue, cyan and green extracted from five areas of the image.*

B: 130
C: 95%
G: 75

B: 200
C: 70%
G: 140

B: 100
C: 80%
G: 95

B: 90
C: 70%
G: 90

B: 80
C: 70%
G: 85

# TREATMENTS

**BLACK AND WHITE**

| | |
|---|---|
| REDS | 40% |
| YELLOWS | 60% |
| GREENS | 40% |
| CYANS | 131% |
| BLUES | 164% |
| MAGENTAS | 80% |

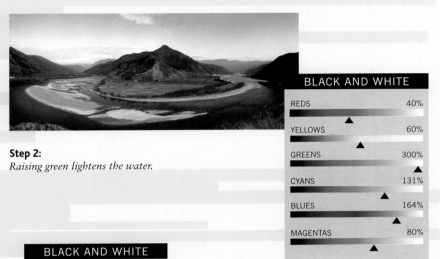

**Step 1**
*Raising blue and cyan together, but favoring blue, lightens and evens out the sky*

**Step 2:**
*Raising green lightens the water.*

**BLACK AND WHITE**

| | |
|---|---|
| REDS | 40% |
| YELLOWS | 60% |
| GREENS | 300% |
| CYANS | 131% |
| BLUES | 164% |
| MAGENTAS | 80% |

**BLACK AND WHITE**

| | |
|---|---|
| REDS | 40% |
| YELLOWS | 60% |
| GREENS | -200% |
| CYANS | 131% |
| BLUES | 164% |
| MAGENTAS | 80% |

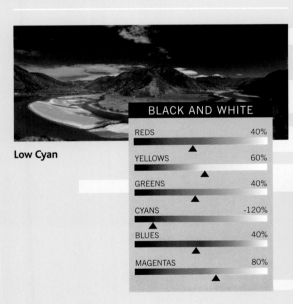

**Low Cyan**

**BLACK AND WHITE**

| | |
|---|---|
| REDS | 40% |
| YELLOWS | 60% |
| GREENS | 40% |
| CYANS | -120% |
| BLUES | 40% |
| MAGENTAS | 80% |

**Step 3**
*Lowering green darkens the water for contrast with the sandbanks.*

**Hi Con**

**BLACK AND WHITE**

| | |
|---|---|
| REDS | 174% |
| YELLOWS | 109% |
| GREENS | -196% |
| CYANS | -88% |
| BLUES | -18% |
| MAGENTAS | 183% |

**BLACK AND WHITE**

| | |
|---|---|
| REDS | 40% |
| YELLOWS | 60% |
| GREENS | 40% |
| CYANS | 60% |
| BLUES | -120% |
| MAGENTAS | 80% |

**Low blue**

**TREATMENTS**

Litchfield church

B: 120
C: 95%
G: 60

B: 200
C: 65%
G: 145

B: 180
C: 65%
G: 150

B: 220
C: 45%
G: 175

B: 160
C: 70%
G: 140

Measurements

## BLACK AND WHITE

| | |
|---|---|
| REDS | 40% |
| YELLOWS | 60% |
| GREENS | -200% |
| CYANS | -60% |
| BLUES | 60% |
| MAGENTAS | 80% |

**Low cyan, mid blue**

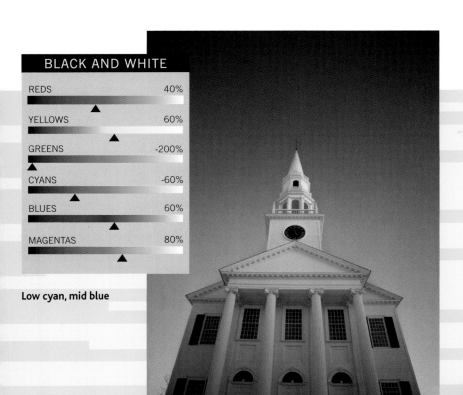

## BLACK AND WHITE

| | |
|---|---|
| REDS | 40% |
| YELLOWS | 60% |
| GREENS | -200% |
| CYANS | -29% |
| BLUES | 116% |
| MAGENTAS | 29% |

## BLACK AND WHITE

| | |
|---|---|
| REDS | 40% |
| YELLOWS | 60% |
| GREENS | 40% |
| CYANS | 90% |
| BLUES | -60% |
| MAGENTAS | 80% |

**Low blue, mid cyan**

**Even sky**

# HANDLING SUBTLETIES

The hue adjustment examples and issues that we've looked at so far have all involved colors that were either distinct, or at least obviously important to control in some way.

I f you look back at many of the previous examples, like the church on page 23, feature strong colors that can be interpreted in wholly different ways using relatively extreme settings in the Black and White tool's six adjustment sliders. Many more picture situations, however, simply contain subtle colors that can be exploited to fine-tune the image—as an alternative to, or in addition to the usual tonal adjustments such as applying contrast curves and tweaking local contrast (such as with Photoshop's Shadows/Highlights method).

Here is just such an example, an image that relies on structure and form much more than color—hence the decision to render it in monochrome. The default conversion is perfectly acceptable, but can still benefit from tweaking. One of the potentials in this image is the geometric pattern of highlights; the backlighting gives an edge not only to

the wooden fencing and structures, but also to the two animals and the farmer. A first step is to raise the yellow component in order to lighten the highlights on the wood and the calf—late in the afternoon, this light is warm. At the same time, the red is taken down to give a little separation in these highlights. The softer, bluer highlights on the buffalo and farmer (they reflect skylight) also give a valuable opportunity to raise them, and so relate them more closely to the other edge-lighting.

Bringing all these edge-lights together, coordinating them as it were, is the key to the processing of this image. Hue adjustment has gone some way toward this. What remains is to selectively increase the contrast of the buffalo and farmer. As they are located in their own, separate region of the frame, a simple gradient selection (using the Quick Mask mode), makes it easy to apply an S-curve that increases their contrast and lightens them slightly. The effect is to make them more similar in tone and contrast to the more strongly lit foreground.

**Color original**
*The original rural view*

**Default desaturation**
*A straight desaturation conversion for comparison*

# PROCESSING

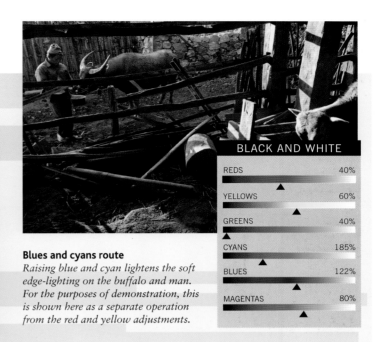

**BLACK AND WHITE**

| | |
|---|---|
| REDS | 40% |
| YELLOWS | 60% |
| GREENS | 40% |
| CYANS | 185% |
| BLUES | 122% |
| MAGENTAS | 80% |

**Blues and cyans route**
*Raising blue and cyan lightens the soft edge-lighting on the buffalo and man. For the purposes of demonstration, this is shown here as a separate operation from the red and yellow adjustments.*

**BLACK AND WHITE**

| | |
|---|---|
| REDS | 10% |
| YELLOWS | 101% |
| GREENS | 40% |
| CYANS | 60% |
| BLUES | 20% |
| MAGENTAS | 80% |

**Reds and yellows route**
*Raising yellow and lowering red strengthens contrast on the parts of the wood that are directly lit and lit by reflection.*

**Combined adjustments**
*The two sets of adjustment shown together.*

**Masked area**
*The gradient tool used in Quick Mask mode to select the upper left part of the frame.*

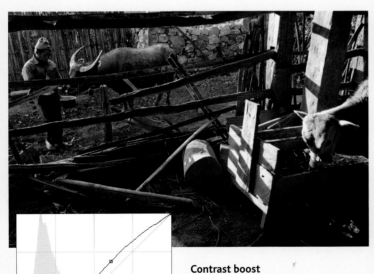

**Contrast boost**
*A curve applied to the selection.*

**Final result with selective contrast**
*The final black-and-white result.*

137

# SECTION 3
# CREATIVE CHOICES

**P**ossibly the greatest difference between photographing in color and photographing in black and white is in expression. There are, of course, all kinds of ways of treating color, made all the easier with the range of software processing no available, but by far the most accepted standard is the target of "realism." Without getting philosophical about what realism means in the context of photography, the normal aims of most people's color photography are to get a result which in terms of image quality are faithful to the original scene. Black and white begins with a quite different premise, as we've seen. It does not, cannot, pretend to realism, and the starting point is the individual photographer's idea of how a scene can look in shades of gray.

This might seem an obvious point to make, but it implies something important—all the choices about how to visualize a scene, shoot, and process are creative. This frees up whole imaginative process, and you can choose to interpret an image in almost any manner. It could be sombre, bright, airy, rich, delicate, soft, harsh, contrasty… the expression and treatment is almost infinitely variable.

Added to this, and stemming partly from it, is the fact that a black-and-white image can be treated to much greater extremes (such as of contrast and key) than can a typical color image. As just one example of this, consider the usual processing limits for a color image, with highlight and shadow clipping being major considerations. Not slipping beyond the limits is fast becoming a rule, even an obsession, in digital processing. But try exceeding the highlight and shadow limits in black and white, as film photographers have done for decades (see the image by Bill Brandt in this chapter), and it will not necessarily look wrong. The latitude for creative expression, in other words, is built into black and white.

# THINKING IN BLACK & WHITE

Nevertheless, underneath, the sensor itself is purely monochrome—it reacts only to the total quantity of multi-spectrum "white" light falling on it from different surfaces and light sources in the scene. This means that, unless you drastically and expensively remove the filter, you always have a color version of the view even if you are fully committed to creating black-and-white imagery.

**The Bayer filter, with its mosaic of green, red, and blue, preserves color information from the scene in front of the camera by separating it into three channels.**

The easiest approach to digital back-and-white, therefore, is to shoot first and later review the images to select those which might work better in monochrome. Absolutely nothing wrong with that, and for obvious reasons of illustration, many of the images in this book were chosen and processed in this kind of workflow. However, "full" black-and-white photography means anticipating, selecting and composing monochrome right from the start. And the only way to do this is to train oneself to think and see in black and white. There are optical aids, as described here, but these are really tricks to fool the eye for a short while into ignoring the color in a scene. More effective long term is constant practice and experience in mentally filtering out color information.

This is not at all fanciful. For many years, serious photographers trained themselves to do just this. Edward Weston, as quoted earlier (page 29), was one of the generation of photographers who grew up shooting black and white, and so "spent years trying to avoid" the temptations of colorful scenes. To succeed in monochrome meant being able to see in advance what would work without color. Eliot Porter, who as we saw moved permanently from black-and-white to color without acquiring the dogmatism of the converted, said that "When Ansel Adams photographs something, he sees it as a black-and-white image right away and so he photographs it that way." That comes from years of training.

From the early and mid-twentieth century American school, artists like Sieglitz, Weston, and Adams took this further than the practical. Adams stressed the importance of "visualization" (deciding at the time of shooting how the final print should look). And this was by not necessarily as it appeared. Adams reiterated Alfred Stieglitz's well-known dictum that the final image (always a monochrome print in those days) should reveal "what you saw and felt." "Once you admit your personal perception or emotional response," he wrote, "the image becomes something more than factual, and you are on the doorstep of an enlarged experience." All of this combined visualizing at a practical level in black and white with the emotional level of how the scene should feel.

A minority of photographers shifted at some point in their careers between black and white and color, among them notably Eliot Porter, Joel Meyerowitz, and Harry Callahan. As you will experience for yourself, moving from one camp to the other heightens awareness of the mental processes involved. Sometimes it is easier to define the skill of seeing in monochrome in comparison to what goes on with color photography. Eliot Porter wrote: "I think it's entirely different from black and white. When photographing subjects like rocks, the approach is entirely different, because in black and white you see the forms much more than you do in color." Answering the question of how important it was to look for color rather than form, he replied, "You don't have to look for it—you see it. I see it as a color image right away—not always, because I still do some black and white. Some of pictures I take in color could just as well have been done in black and white."

In their classic *A Concise History of Photography*, Helmut and Alison Gernsheim declared that, "Good color photography demands more of the photographer than simply shooting with color film. Compared with black and white, color requires not only a different technique but a different way of seeing. In monochrome the massing of light and shade and the reproduction of texture are of the utmost importance."

**Garrapata Beach, 1954**
*Photograph by Brett Weston*
© *The Brett Weston Archive*
*brettwestonarchive.com*

# THINKING IN BLACK & WHITE

## PERCEPTUAL AIDS

### MONOCHROME VIEWING FILTER

One of the oldest devices for helping to see in black and white is the Kodak Wratten 90 monochrome viewing filter, designed to handicap the eye. A dark grayish-amber in color, it does two things. First, by darkening the view it throws the eye's response for a few moments toward the rods rather than the cones. Second, its amber tint counters the eye's extra sensitivity toward yellow-green.

**Wratten 90**

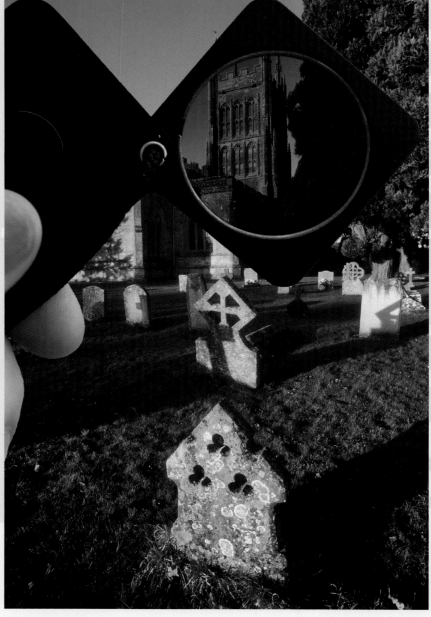

**Wratten 90 in use**

CREATIVE CHOICES

## MONOCHROME LIVE-VIEW

Cameras which offer a live preview (increasingly common among DSLRs) together with a black-and-white screen view, give a true and useful preview of how an image will look in monochrome. This is, as you would expect, a simple desaturation, and ignores the many channel-mixing possibilities during processing.

THINKING IN BLACK & WHITE

143

# THE RANGE OF LIGHT: ANSEL ADAMS & THE WESTONS

t is apparent as a desire to capture the full range (Yosemite and the Range of Light, a mild pun, was indeed the title of one of his books) and a leaning toward drama, with rich blacks balanced against just-discernible high-value textures in snow, clouds and the water spray.

Edward Weston, friend of Adams and sharing many of the same views about rich tonality and an

**There is a common aesthetic running through most of Adams' prints**

"honesty" to both form and content that was a rejection of Pictorialism, worked primarily with large negatives and contact printing. His best known images span much the same full range

as those of Adams, although the latter felt compelled to write that "Edward Weston's prints are much 'quieter' than many realize." They both agreed on the need to envision the print at the time they were shooting, and that this final image—first in the mind, then on paper—should be personal to the photographer. As Weston put it, "the ultimate end, the print, is but a duplication of all that I saw and felt through my camera," although the word 'but' is unduly modest. Brett, his son, continued in the same tradition, with perhaps even more emphasis on tonal drama, while never pushing the limits of full black and empty white.

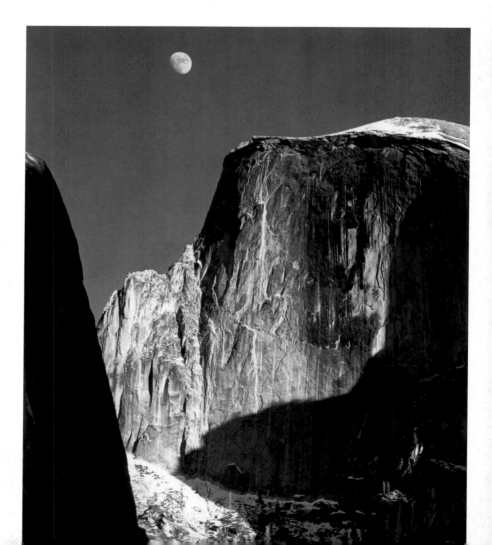

**Moon and half dome**
© *Ansel Adams*

**Juniper Lake (Opposite)**
© *Edward Weston*

# THE LONG RANGE OF GRAY:PAUL STRAND

**T**his reflected both their preferred subject matter and an aesthetic in which subtle nuances between gray tones, well distinguished one from another, were highly regarded. One of the exemplars of this approach, at least for the majority of his long career, was Paul Strand, one of the twentieth century's most famous photographers. Strand's work covers 60 years, from 1914 until his death in 1976, and he made all his own prints until the very end, when he took an assistant to work under his guidance.

Unexpectedly, two of Strand's best-known images, *Wall Street* from 1915 and *White Fence* from 1916, are full of strong contrast and not at all typical of the bulk of his prints. He drew back from this dramatic approach, and his many portraits have almost all the attention concentrated in the middle range. The skin tones of his subjects are noticeably well modulated. The reason for this change is linked to the materials he used, for as we shall see in the last chapter, Strand began with platinum printing, as did many photographers of his generation. The tonal quality of a platinum print is so different from the silver bromide printing that succeeded it and which became the known standard for black and white, that it represented almost a unique medium in its own right. Dating back to the 1830s, platinotypes, as they are also called, have a deposit of platinum that sits mainly on the paper's surface, as opposed to a silver print in which the image-forming silver lies in a gelatin coating. While the deepest platinum blacks are not as black as those in a silver print (which has a higher D-Max, in technical terms), the tonal separation within the range is remarkable. In particular, midtones appear expanded, and a large amount of detail is visible in the shadows. While there is no satisfactory way of simulating this in a digital image, the ideal of good separation and a long tonal range can still be pursued.

When converting, as below, it helps the effect *not* to close up both black and white points, and then to lower the contrast. Visually this forces more attention to the midtones. The methods used here are first to use hue adjustment to bring tones closer together (for example, see what lowering the yellow does to the out-of-focus background at upper right), and then to apply a traditional contrast-reducing curve overall.

**While in no way suggesting that Adams and Weston paid any less attention to the central midtones than to the ends of the range, other photographer-printers dwelled much more on the grays, from dark-gray to light-gray.**

CREATIVE CHOICES

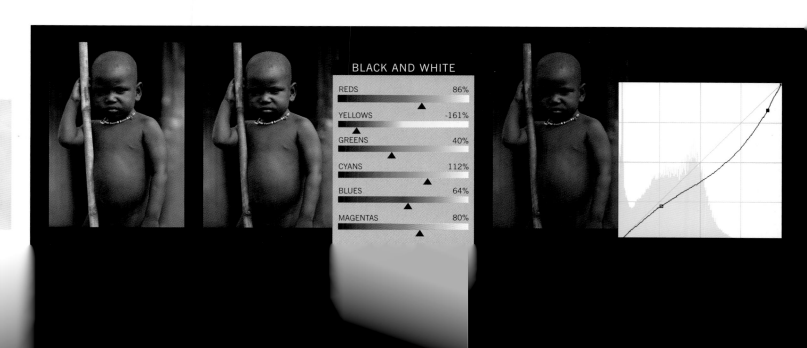

BLACK AND WHITE

| | |
|---|---|
| REDS | 86% |
| YELLOWS | -161% |
| GREENS | 40% |
| CYANS | 112% |
| BLUES | 64% |
| MAGENTAS | 80% |

**Paul Strand:** *The Family*, Luzzara, Italy 1953
© *Aperture foundation, Inc., Paul Strand Archive*

# MIDTONES

**Midtones define themselves, but it's as well to remember that this is a commonsense definition and does not lend itself to precise figures and levels.**

Midtones simply mean the usually large middle of the brightness range, everything except the shadows and the highlights. For more precision we need to go to the Zone System, but the significance of the term "midtone" lies in the way we see and perceive. The human eye adapts wonderfully and rapidly to changes in brightness, but still, within any one range of tones, will tend to settle on the middle. Metering systems, and most photographers unconsciously, do the same with exposure. In a straightforward, single-subject image, a clear subject of attention tends to look "right" when it is rendered in midtones. Most of us follow this so naturally that it seems too obvious to mention, but it is fundamental. And it is even more true of a monochrome image than in color, as a striking hue in the highlights or shadows can catch the attention, deliberately or otherwise. A rich sunset, for example, draws more attention to the highlights in a color image.

There's no need to be obsessive when you are setting the limits, and as both these examples show, many images resolve themselves easily into shadows, midtones, and highlights. In the case of the cheetah, the animal is so obviously the only subject that the shadows (darker recesses of the tree) and highlights (over-exposed background) exist only for the composition—details within them would be irrelevant, and even distract from the animal. As we've seen elsewhere, black and white allows more extreme processing than does color, without looking "wrong." In a case like this, clipping in shadows and highlights would be perfectly acceptable.

**Exploded layers view**
*Exploded layers separate this image into shadow, midtone, and highlight.*

CREATIVE CHOICES

148

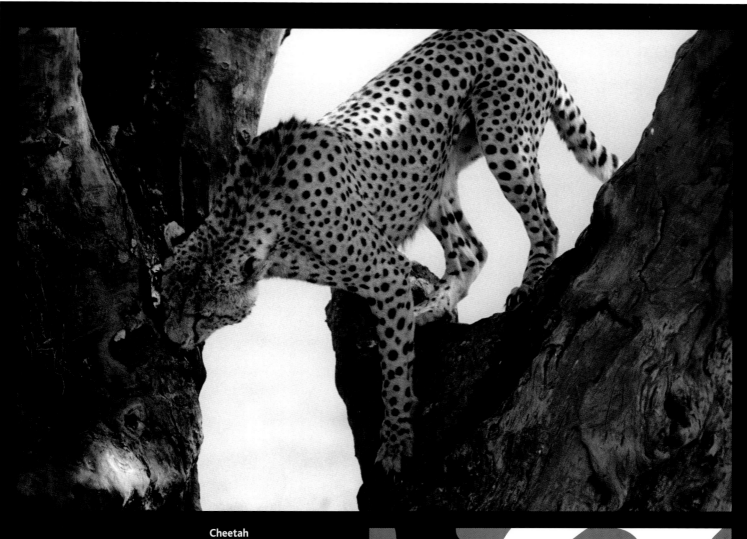

**Cheetah**
*Typically, midtones coincide
with the main subject of
interest, especially in
monochrome.*

# CONTRAST HIGH

**Black and white lends itself to high-contrast treatment much more so than does color, for two reasons.**

One is that monochrome is not held in check by the expectation that it is a faithful and realistic version of things, as we saw on pages 58-61 Interpretation. The other is that increasing contrast is a particularly good way of emphasizing structure and form—and these are key qualities in black-and-white photography. The traditional S-curve that raises the lower highlights and lowers the mid-shadows is the standard tool for raising contrast globally, across the image. By choosing how high or low to put the points that you drag, and by adding more than two points, it can be fine-tuned for subtly different results. Nevertheless, in the face of newer processing tools and more time-consuming methods, it is a little crude. This is fine for many, even the majority of images, possibly, but by no means always the ideal.

Here we look at a more considered way of selectively increasing contrast, using a variety of tools, on two images. The first, on these two pages, is at a Dinka cattle camp in southern Sudan, and while the color image is workmanlike, it seemed that it had potential as a high-contrast image in black and white. In particular, there is the play between the black and white of the foreground cow, the correspondence between the curve of its shoulder and neck and that of the other animal's horns, and the skin of the young cowherd.

However, adjusting the hues offer two opposing contrasts. In one, the first here, lowering yellow and maximising green, cyan and blue gives the highest contrast with the out-of-focus background. The second choice, maximising yellow and red, gives the greatest contrast in the lower half of the frame. One possibility, therefore, was to do both separately, and then blend the two versions manually, as shown here. Broad strokes, erasing one layer over another, are sufficient. Following this, a fairly strong use of Photoshop's Shadows/Highlights control increase local contrast.

**Original**
*Color original*

**Finished**
*The final, selectively high contrast, result*

# WORKFLOW

**BLACK AND WHITE**

| | |
|---|---|
| REDS | -31% |
| YELLOWS | -62% |
| GREENS | 300% |
| CYANS | 300% |
| BLUES | 300% |
| MAGENTAS | 51% |

**Hue adjustment 1**
*Raising cool colors, lowering warm ones.*

**Hue adjustment 2**
*Raising yellow and red tones.*

**BLACK AND WHITE**

| | |
|---|---|
| REDS | 198% |
| YELLOWS | 300% |
| GREENS | 40% |
| CYANS | 60% |
| BLUES | 20% |
| MAGENTAS | 80% |

**Erasing layer**
*The first version overlaid on the second, and partially erased.*

**SHADOWS/HIGHLIGHTS**

**SHADOWS**

| | |
|---|---|
| AMOUNT | 8% |
| TONAL WIDTH | 76% |
| RADIUS | 54px |

**HIGHLIGHTS**

| | |
|---|---|
| AMOUNT | 35% |
| TONAL WIDTH | 7% |
| RADIUS | 30px |

**ADJUSTMENTS**

| | |
|---|---|
| COLOR CORRECTION | +20 |
| MIDTONE CONTRAST | +52 |
| BLACK CLIP | 0.01% |
| WHITE CLIP | 0.01% |

**Shadows/Highlights**
*Shadows/Highlight settings to emphasize mid-range contrast.*

**Blended**
*The finished manual blend.*

CONTRAST HIGH

# CONTRAST HIGH

This image has been chosen to make a direct comparison between two ways of heightening contrast. The overall results are similar but the specifics very different. The scene is a bus terminal in Cartagena, Colombia, the sunlight strong and low, the color red! The aim, in converting to monochrome, is to convey this intensity in the absence of the rich red. Step one is to make the usual default conversion as a benchmark, and work from that.

The standard method would be to apply an S-curve, as shown here, and the result is good. But now let's try and achieve the same overall degree of contrast in a different way, by adjusting only the hues. The obvious approach is to go far a bright red, so

although there are few cool tones in this late afternoon scene, we can take cyan and blue down to their minima. Next, we raise the red slider until just before the side of the bus goes to featureless white—we still want some hint of detail. The result is high contrast to the same degree as with the S-curve, but with a different distribution of tones—though strange if you knew the starting point were red.

We can also go for the opposite conversion, a dark red. Lowering the red slider does this, but also, because the entire scene is diffused with warm sunlight, it darkens everything. The solution is simple—raise the yellow slider to lighten overall while still leaving the red dark.

**Original**
*In the original the bus is a striking red.*

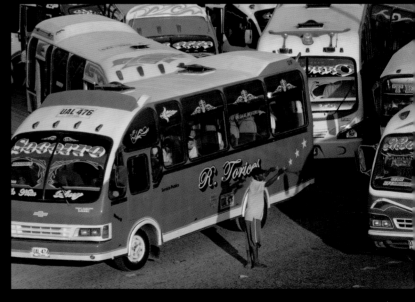

**Deaturated**
*Default conversion in Photoshop.*

# CONVERSION ALTERNATIVES

**High Contrast Curve**
*A conventional image-editor S-curve and the high-contrast result.*

| BLACK AND WHITE | |
| --- | --- |
| REDS | -100% |
| YELLOWS | 60% |
| GREENS | 40% |
| CYANS | 60% |
| BLUES | 20% |
| MAGENTAS | 80% |

**Low red 1**
*Lowering red for maximum dark rendering.*

| BLACK AND WHITE | |
| --- | --- |
| REDS | 155% |
| YELLOWS | 60% |
| GREENS | 40% |
| CYANS | -200% |
| BLUES | -200% |
| MAGENTAS | 80% |

**High red**
*Red is raised as high as possible without clipping.*

| BLACK AND WHITE | |
| --- | --- |
| REDS | -100% |
| YELLOWS | 220% |
| GREENS | 40% |
| CYANS | 60% |
| BLUES | 20% |
| MAGENTAS | 80% |

**Low red 2**
*As "low red 1", but the yellow is raised for an overall lighter look.*

# CONTRAST LOW

**Continuing the interpretation, theme, in which black-and-white imagery can be given wide range of treatments, certain classes of scene respond well to a low-contrast approach.**

Of course, any scene can be lowered in contrast, and it ultimately depends on the vision of the particular photographer, but some picture situations are obvious candidates. Fog, mist, rain, indeed any softening effect from atmosphere, has a certain evocative appeal, and maintaining it means essentially keeping your hands off the black and white points. The histogram accompanying the as-shot image of trees in Dedham Vale, England shows just how much space can typically be found on either side of the tonal range. Low-contrast images like this tend to sit well inside the scale, with no blacks and no whites. This gives a great deal of latitude for exposure and key, meaning that in this case increasing exposure by about a stop would simply shift the histogram to the right without any clipping, and decreasing by the same amount would do the reverse.

One way of reducing the contrast further would be to lower the red slider, given the reddishness that suffuses the original color image, from the just-risen sun. Or, there is always the temptation to close up the black and white points, as shown here. This really is a matter of taste, and many people would prefer this, though not me. This deserves a warning—digital practice has introduced photographers to technical tools such as the histogram, adjustable curves, black and white points, which is all to the good, but it has also created some automatic responses, which is not so good. Most careful photographers check the black and white points in an image, but the unthinking reaction of closing them up exactly to just below clipping does no favors to a photograph that deserves to be delicate and nuanced.

**Low contrast scene**
*Typical of the landscapes that inspired generations of Chinese artists working with brush and ink, limestone peaks and pillars glimpsed through shifting clouds around the summit of Huangshizai in Hunan.*

# LOW CONTRAST CONVERSION

### Dedham Vale
*The color original, bathed in the warm tones of sunrise.*

| BLACK AND WHITE | |
|---|---|
| REDS | -49% |
| YELLOWS | 60% |
| GREENS | 40% |
| CYANS | 60% |
| BLUES | 20% |
| MAGENTAS | 80% |

### Default
*The default conversion*

### Low res
*Reduced red component further reduces contrast*

### Contrast-enhanced
*Default with points closed in*
*For comparison, the default conversion with black and white points closed in.*

# INTO SHADOW & DARKNESS: BILL BRANDT & DON MCCULLIN

T he reasons for wanting to do this vary from a love of the richness of heavy blacks to trying to match the mood of serious, even threatening subject matter, or even reflecting the mood of the photographer. Two photographers in particular stand out: Bill Brandt, who photographed Britain from the 1930s through the 1960s, creating a number of iconic images, and Don McCullin, best known for his war photographs from Cyprus to Beirut, but who then turned his attention to landscape.

In both cases, there seems to have been a progression over time toward printing darker. In the case of Brandt, his wife said of his pictures of buildings in Newcastle that they "looked to him as if they might have been built of coal." It also tended to fit quite well with his obvious liking for strongly geometrical compositions—these normally lend themselves to high-contrast treatment.

Don McCullin recognises in his dark, heavy printing a reflection of his childhood and career, writing, "[M]y eyes had grown accustomed to the dark. All I saw seemed to echo my childhood and the scenes of deprivation, dereliction, death and disaster, smashed minds, and broken bodies, that I had witnessed in other countries." This preference has been transferred to his current landscape photography of his home in Somerset, in the south-west of England. In an interview with broadcaster John Tulsa, he said, " I look forward to the evening light, and the naked trees when I go out; and I live in this Arthurian world of Somerset." In many ways, McCullin's later work exemplifies the idea of the expressive print, full of personal feeling.

**A very different aesthetic of printing from the essentially "straight" and "pure" style promoted by Edward Weston and the other Californians is the sombre low key of heavily inked images, with midtones pushed down so that most of the detail has to be read in low values.**

**Harold Pinter**
*© Bill Brandt*

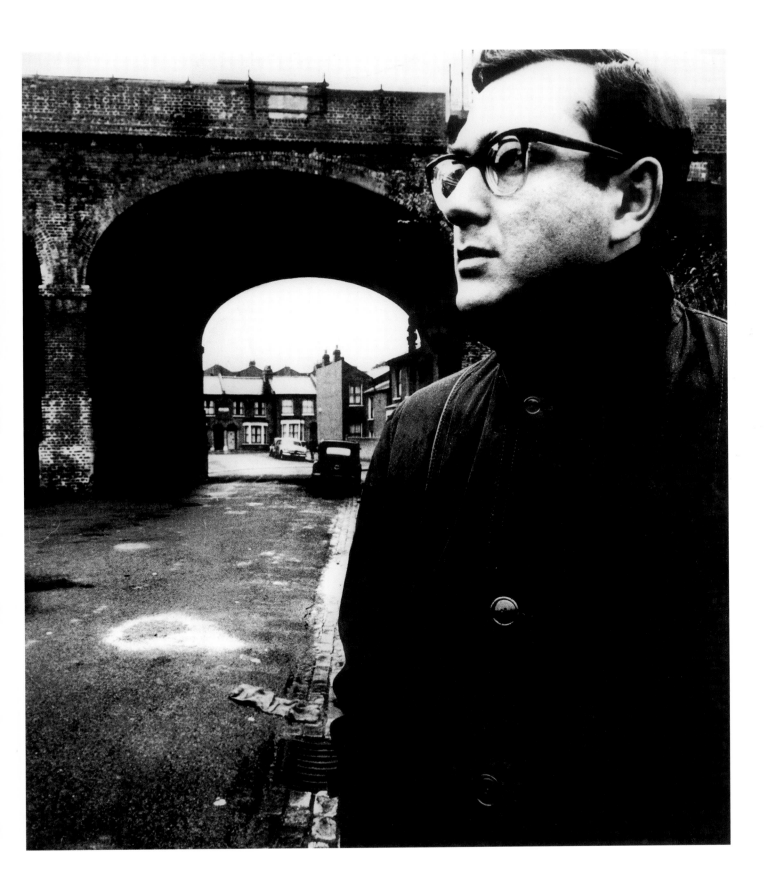

# LOW KEY

**I**deal conditions are when a large area of the frame, even most of it, is in shadow, when most of these shadow areas carry no essential detail, and when there is a structure of lighter tones to make a contrast. Indeed, contrast, if only on a finely detailed scale, contributes greatly to the success of many low-key images. But, as with all special treatments, from infrared to high-key, simply following a formula of "this is a low-key kind of image" misses the point. What matters is how you, as an individual photographer, see the scene and the potential in it.

**While a darker key can be applied to any image, according to the mood of the photographer, certain kinds of lighting and scene lend themselves more readily to this treatment than others.**

This example is reasonably conventional for low key—the setting is a dark interior, with weak side-lighting that reveals enough of the subject to make it obvious, and a background that can easily go to black. And probably should go to black in order to keep attention on the texture of skin and beard. The histogram that you can see when we make the Levels adjustment is typical of a mainly-dark image with low-key potential. The first step with this image in order to strengthen the low-key effect is to make the background as black as possible, though without losing important shadow detail on the man and his hat. In Photoshop Levels, holding down ⌥/Alt key as you click on and drag the black point slider shows the amount of clipping, and updates it as you adjust the slider. Normally with an image we would pull back from this to avoid clipping, but in this case some solid black is exactly what is wanted. In order to keep the midtones more or less as they were, it helps in this case to raise the mid-point slider by approximately the same amount as the black point has been closed in—from 1.00 to 1.20.

This is as far as we need to go, but there is still plenty of room for adjusting the white point or the mid-point to taste. And, of course, there is always the option of using the hue sliders to alter tonal relationships and contrast. Here there are two alternative versions, one to maximize the contrast between beard and skin, the other to minimize it. By now, the procedure should be predictable and straightforward. For the former, lowering red and yellow darkens the skin, raising cyan and blue whitens the beard. For the opposite effect, doing the reverse makes it possible to blend the beard in with the skin until it is almost unnoticeable—if that were wanted.

**Dark skin**
*The color original, with brown in the skin and some cyan and blue in the white beard.*

# ADJUSTMENTS

**Default**
*The default conversion.*

**Shadow clip**
*Closing in the black point, which invovles holding down the ⌥/Alt key to view clipping as you adjust the levels sliders.*

| BLACK AND WHITE | |
|---|---|
| REDS | 16% |
| YELLOWS | -14% |
| GREENS | 40% |
| CYANS | 122% |
| BLUES | 120% |
| MAGENTAS | 80% |

| BLACK AND WHITE | |
|---|---|
| REDS | 116% |
| YELLOWS | 110% |
| GREENS | 40% |
| CYANS | -150% |
| BLUES | -152% |
| MAGENTAS | 80% |

**Emphasise beard**
*The settings to lighten the beard and darken the skin.*

**Knock back beard**
*The settings to blend the beard tones into those of the skin.*

LOW KEY

159

# HIGH-KEY & GRAPHIC: HARRY CALLAHAN & EIKOH HOSOE

High-key meant rationing the light from the enlarger and, in order to accentuate the few parts of the image allowed to remain in what is essentially a field of white, applying extensive local control—that is, dodging and burning-in. The digital equivalent of this takes pace in image-editing programs such as Photoshop, but a custom profile for the printer can also be made to accentuate the contrast and whiteness.

**If style can be pushed toward darkness and shadows, as on the previous pages, it can also go in the other direction.**

Harry Callahan, 1912-1999, is known for his frequent use of high-key printing. Callahan's work changed direction after he met Ansel Adams in 1941, following which he adapted some of Adams' ideas. From this point on he added to his repertoire high-key abstractions such as Weeds in Snow, and certain portraits of his wife Eleanor (there were many, in different styles) in which her skin is rendered white and, in one instance, appears in silhouette emerging from almost-white water. For high-key to work visually, it demands high contrast with the few remaining dark tones, and this inevitably leads to a graphic style. By this I mean imagery in which lines and points, the rawest graphic forms, dominate, while tonal gradation is suppressed. This in turn creates abstractions, often puzzling at first (as in Callahan's photograph of the uneven, cross-like creases formed by Eleanor's legs and buttocks, which at first glance resembles his other images of abstracted weeds and grasses set against white skies or white snow). Clearly, this aesthetic appeals to a certain kind of personality, in which content is subordinated to form.

One important area of decision is whether or not to allow the edges of the image, by definition and intention extremely pale, bleed into the surrounding paper. At one extreme, this effectively makes the image borderless, which can make for an interesting discussion in itself. The more traditional approach has been to hold the brightest tone a noticeable level darker than pure paper white, in order to hold the limits of the image, but the balance is a fine one, because too far below white runs the risk of looking muddy. This issue extends to mounting and framing, as the eye of the viewer is inevitably affected by the difference in tone. One of Callahan's solutions to this was to frame the image in black—either the black of the film rebate or a printed-in black edge.

Japanese photographer Eikoh Hosoe, born in 1933, has made particularly strong use of dodging and burning-in to create his expressive prints that are frequently very high in contrast. His frequent use of areas of pure white, notably in his series of close-ups of the bodies of men and women juxtaposed and in images taken for the book Kamaitachi, have a direct connection with the tradition of the Japanese woodcut. In traditional Ukiyo-e prints, a proportion of which is erotic, men are often depicted with dark skin, women with white, in deliberate contrast.

**High key**
*This portrait is exposed so that almost all the detail is in the right half of the histogram, showing in the light gray tonality.*

**Very high key**
*This shot uses a curve to exaggerate the already high key shot to the point that its tone is reminicient of Harry Callahan's famous "Eleanor" shot.*

# HIGH KEY

**M**ore fundamentally, for high-key to work well, there usually needs to be some smaller darker elements that are integral to the image. Raising the brightness and contrast throws emphasis on whatever smaller darker areas remain. Both of the examples here, in different ways, rely on this feature—small key subjects in an expansive white setting.

**As we saw from the previous pages, a high-key treatment depends on a large area and high value of whiteness, and on high contrast.**

This first image, dawn over the Altausseer lake in Ausria's Salzkammergut region, actually works well in color, and was shot that way. Nevertheless, it lends itself to this other, high-key treatment. Critical to the image is that the fisherman in his small boat is seen against only the reflections of the mountains in the still water, not against the mountains themselves. The position of the boat in the frame and its size add to the delayed reaction in seeing it and consequently the "inversion" of the landscape. Making a high key version, we should keep this in mind.

At this time of day, the mountains and sky in the reflection are bathed in blue, and so can be lightened and darkened, while the low mist is more white. Simply then, raising the blue strongly, with cyan and red to a lesser degree (both are present in the bluish cast), whitens the image overall without affecting the rowing boat. In one stroke we already have a high-key effect. The histogram is typical, and the reverse of the low-key one on page 158. But we can take this further, by closing in the black and white points to enhance the contrast. Simply doing this operation, however, also lowers the midtones, and to keep them high, the mid-point slider can be raised, here quite strongly from 1.00 to 1.70.

Finally, there is always the option to go to a high-key extreme by clipping some of the whites. This would normally never do in color, nor usually in normal black-and-white processing. The result is a matter of opinion, but valid in that it draws even more attention to the man in his boat.

**Altausseer See**
*The color original, suffused in dawn blue light*

# CONVERSIONS

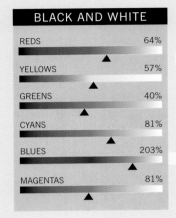

| | |
|---|---|
| REDS | 64% |
| YELLOWS | 57% |
| GREENS | 40% |
| CYANS | 81% |
| BLUES | 203% |
| MAGENTAS | 81% |

*Hue adjustment to whiten the blues*

**Initial conversion**
*The monochrome,
high-key version.*

*The typical high-key histogram, but
with space remaining on the right.*

**Contrast**
*Closing up
the end-points
heightens the
contrast.*

▲ 60    ▲ 1.00    △ 236

**Closing up**
*With the addition of
raising the mid-point
keeps the image white.*

▲ 57    ▲ 1.70    △ 235

**Extreme**
*An extreme version,
deliberately clipping
some of the highlights.*

▲ 60    ▲ 1.85    △ 222

HIGH KEY

# HIGH KEY

**H**ere, hue adjustment will be integral, but to demonstrate the point, let's begin with the more standard method using Levels. The dead twigs and flowers are yellow, and so quite pale—not really much of a shot in color. Nevertheless, closing in the black and white points at least gets us to a very white image. However, beginning with hue adjustment, the straw-colored

**This second example, twigs in snow, could have been tailor-made for a high-key conversion.**

twigs contrast with the bluish hint to the snow, so that pulling the hue sliders in opposite directions quickly gets us to a high-key result with strong contrast. The Photoshop preset High Contrast Blue is similar.

High-key being a fairly popular treatment, some processing software offers presets that aim for the same thing. The three shown here are "Creative Black and White: High Contrast" from LightRoom, "Black and White: High Contrast" from DxO Optics Pro, and "Black and White: High Key Portrait" from LightZone.

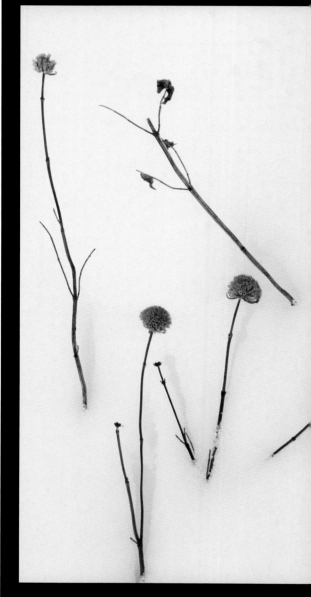

**Color original**
*The color original, quite low in contrast on an overcast day*

# HIGH KEY COMPARISONS

### Default
*The default conversion, with histogram, which shows that there is still room for adjustment at both ends of the scale, hence not strongly high key*

40      3.01                    244

*Closing in the white point and strongly raising the mid-point gives a high-key result with just moderate contrast*

| BLACK AND WHITE | |
|---|---|
| REDS | 21% |
| YELLOWS | -85% |
| GREENS | 40% |
| CYANS | 118% |
| BLUES | 131% |
| MAGENTAS | 80% |

### High contrast blue
*Photoshop's High Contrast Blue settings do much the same thing as my "High contrast" ones in this case.*

### High contrast
*Starting again from the color original, lowering the warm tones and raising the cool tones arrives directly at a high-key, high-contrast result.*

| BLACK AND WHITE | |
|---|---|
| PRESET:  High Contrast Blue Filter | |
| REDS | 21% |
| YELLOWS | -85% |
| GREENS | 40% |
| CYANS | 118% |
| BLUES | 131% |
| MAGENTAS | 80% |

*Three preset high-key conversions from specific software: LighRoom, DxO OPtics Pro and LightZone.*

**Lightroom**

**DxO**

**LightZone**

# DIGITAL ZONE SYSTEM

**Ansel Adams et al's Zone System never seems to go away, despite the fact that it was invented for a highly specific kind of photography that very few people ever practised— namely black-and-white sheet film used for subjects over which the photographer could muse and ponder without being in a rush.**

Such is the power of belief in old masters. The fundamental question for using it in digital photography is not how but why. I'll admit that I'm treating it here out of a sense of duty, and also because if you are a committed black-and-white photographer you will expect to see it here. Nevertheless, frankly it has little value in its original intended way, which was not simply to place a key tone in a particular zone and then see how the other tones would fall, but then to adjust the exposure and processing if needed. This was perfectly possible with a single sheet of black-and-white film, usually impractical with a roll of film, and pointless with digital capture.

That said, it is, as we will see, a useful way of thinking about and assessing scenes and images. This is all to the good, as I suspect that many photographers believe anyway that it is just a tool for analysis, and either skip or have never heard of its practical use in developing a negative. It's worth reviewing this, in order to put the Zone System in proper perspective for digital shooting. The basic procedure involved first measuring the range of brightness in the scene, then choosing a key tone, seeing how everything else would reproduce relative to that key tone, and then making the exposure in anticipation of pushing or pulling the development. I use the term pushing to mean forcing development, to give something similar to the result of using a higher ISO film. Pulling means the opposite, reducing development. The actual techniques are unimportant for us here, but generally involved raising or lowering the temperature of the developer, and increasing or reducing the development time. More important from the point of view of the Zone System was that altering the development also alters the contrast. Crudely put, pushing increases contrast, pulling flattens it.

In practice, this meant that, in the terminology of the Zone System, you chose your important tone and placed it in a particular zone. All the the other tones then fell into various zones. If that created a problem, such as shadow areas that were too dark (in too low a zone), you would adjust the development to expand or compress the contrast. This adjustment of contrast through development is meaningless for digital photography. It was also, incidentally, meaningless for most 35mm or rollfilm shooting, as the altered development would affect every other frame, and was designed for sheet film.

Now, as all of this is completely unnecessary in digital photography, where the processing tools are much more sophisticated and flexible, it remains to treat the Zone System as an evaluation system. In this it continues to shine. The table opposite is crucial, because it assigns meaning to tones. And while every tone has some importance, certain zones are typically critical, particularly Zones III (textured shadow), V (midtones), and VII (textured brights).

*Irrespective of how bright or dark you decide to shoot a scene like this, it contains blocks of tones that relate to each other, some more important to the image than others. This assessment and treatment of a brightly lit scene in clear weather is conventional in its exposure and contrast. Key zones to hold are the sections of*

*whitewashed wall, placed at Zone VIII, which is the maximum before clipping occurs. They contain within them no important detail other than the barest hint of texture, and so do not need to be Zone VII (textured highlights.*

## THE ZONES

An alternative version of the Zone System has 11 zones instead of the 10 shown here, and yet another has 9. Note that we show two versions of the scale here, one of solid tones, the other with an added texture. One school of thought holds that textured zones are closer to the reality of a scene, and so easier to judge.

| | |
|---|---|
| ZONE 0 | Solid, maximum black. 0,0,0 in RGB. No detail. In digital photography, the black point goes here. |
| ZONE I | Almost black, as in deep shadows. No discernible texture. In digital photography, almost solid black. |
| ZONE II | First hint of texture in a shadow. Mysterious, only just visible. In digital photography, the point at which detail begins to be distinguished from noise. |
| ZONE III | TEXTURED SHADOW. A key zone in many scenes and images. Texture and detail are clearly seen, such as the folds and weave of a dark fabric. |
| ZONE IV | Typical shadow value, as in dark foliage, buildings, landscapes. |
| ZONE V | Midtone. The pivotal value. Average, mid-gray, an 18% gray card. Dark skin, light foliage |
| ZONE VI | Average Caucasian skin, concrete in overcast light, shadows on snow in sunlit scenes |
| ZONE VII | TEXTURED BRIGHTS. Pale skin, light-toned and brightly lit concrete. Yellows, pinks and other obviously light colors. In digital photography, the point at which detail can just be seen in highlights. |
| ZONE VIII | The last hint of texture, bright white. In digital photography, the brightest acceptable highlight. |
| ZONE IX | Solid white, 255,255,255 in RGB. Acceptable for specular highlights only. In digital photography, the white point goes here. |

DIGITAL ZONE SYSTEM

167

# DIGITAL ZONE SYSTEM

In this first image, of the Temple of Luxor at sunrise, we can make an initial at-a-glance assessment. For me, this would be that the overall range of sunlit sandstone (a light brownish orange in this light and in color) should be somewhat lighter than a midtone, simply on the grounds that the eye expects a certain degree of brightness from clear sunlight—brighter than average. Also that the sky needs to be a touch less than pure white—there would certainly be no excuse for clipping it to blank white, not least because in a print or on a white web page, the top right corner would bleed off into the surroundings, or need a frame line. Also that all the shadows areas other than the very deepest small ones should "read," with discernible detail, but not be so light that they would take attention away from the lit areas.

In many picture situations, this is all that there is time for, but assuming that the camera is framed and locked down on the tripod, and that there is nothing unexpected about to happen (such as an imminent invasion by a bus-load of tourists), we can assess further in the true Zone System manner. To simplify matters, I've converted the scene into a simplified version in which each solid block of tone is approximately one stop different from the next lighter or darker tone. Note that at this stage (supposed to be at the time of setting up the camera), the actual values are not set and can be shifted higher or lower. Later, digitally, they can also be changed relative to each other during processing, an action not anticipated by the inventors of the Zone System and which invalidates the System as a practical processing tool (though not as an evaluation tool).

The classic procedure, needing plenty of time, is to have already made and printed your own zone scale, from solid black to pure white. This is easy enough to do with a digital printer, although achieving a dense black at the bottom of the scale is a challenge. A glossy paper helps to extend the range perceptually, for the reasons explained on pages 196-199. Armed with this scale (the numbers printed on it shown in the examples are not necessary, but included here to avoid any confusion), the dedicated Zone System photographer can then hold it at arm's length against the scene about to be photographed, and try to match key zones on the scale to those in the scene.

This procedure is represented here. My first concern has to do with the shadows, because while the midtones in general will need to be fine-tuned, they can more or less take care of themselves in any reasonable exposure. As the large statue is the natural first focus of attention, the shadow areas below the knees, and on the side of the face, assume a particular significance. I want them to read, but not that obviously. From the zone scale assessment, I think they should be somewhere between Zone II and III. And incidentally, it has not escaped attention that the seated figures of the two watchmen at lower right give a sense of scale and it would be ideal if they caught viewers' attention—but not immediately. That would suggest having them at Zone I against a local background of Zone II.

Next, we can check the sunlit areas of sandstone. Moving the scale over them, we can see that they cover three $f$-stops of tone. Because they are lit by sharp sunlight, I think they should overall appear brighter than average in the final version, so a reasonable and safe way of deciding this is to find the darkest area of sunlit stone and place that at Zone V. With this decision taken, all the other zones fall into place satisfactorily. The Zone System proves useful in analyzing the scene and reaching this decision, but were there to be any relative adjustments, such as raising a shadow area without raising everything else, I would do it with any of the several digital procedures that we've looked at already; the Zone System would have no part to play in this. This image was chosen, naturally, for its not needing any special processing.

## ZONING

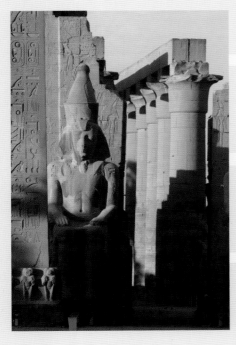

The Temple of Luxor at sunrise, a full-range scene with the focus of attention falling naturally on the sunlit areas of stone, especially the seated statue.

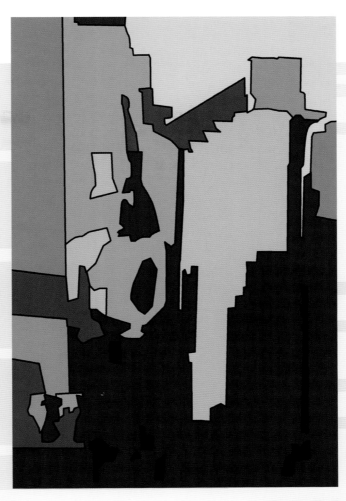

**Blocks**
For convenience, the scene translated into blocked-in segments.

**Finding 1**
*Finding Zones II to III.*

**Finding 2**
*Looking for Zone V—midtones.*

## ZONING CONTINUED

**Original image**
*For reference.*

**Brightness segments**
At the chosen exposure, these are the brightness measurements for the average of each segment.

**Zones**
*The brightness of each segment translated into numbered zones.*

CREATIVE CHOICES

One processing tool that deserves special attention in this context, because it uses a form of the Zone System as a way not just of displaying the tonal values in an image, but of altering their tonal relationships. LightZone's method of what it calls zone mapping comes as close as possible to making digital use of the Zone System.

As with the Zone System itself, the method is at its most intelligible on monochrome images, as displayed here. The key zones appeared to be the open shadows on walls and floor (if treated as such, they would have to be placed at Zone IV "typical shadow value"), the sky, the far facing wall (which would need to be kept well-separated from the sky), and the foreground tree trunk. The one change I would have liked to make to the image given an exposure for this zone placement was the degree of shadow detail on the foreground tree trunk. To help assess how much more visible detail would be best, also shown here is a series of exposures, one stop apart, of the center of the image. From this, I can see that a little less than one extra stop for the tree trunk would be ideal for me.

In LightZone, the ZoneMapper is divided into 16 zones, and rolling the cursor over these shows in the thumbnail at upper right which regions of the image they represent. This makes it easy to locate the zone responsible for the middle of the tree trunk. Dragging this to expand it allows a selective raising of its tonal value.

## KEY BRIGHTS

Because of digital sensors' linear response to light, the highlights are critical in many, maybe most, images. Certainly, accurately assessing the top values in an image is a key skill, and Zone System thinking can help here. In this example, rows of whitewashed pagodas in Mandalay, Burma, the sunlit white is the key tone in the photograph, and from the Zone System needs to be Zone VIII—"last hint of texture." The next most important tone is the light shadow that appears on the far left of the left-hand pagoda, just below the center. This tone also appears in the middle of the center and right rows of pagodas, and is about one zone (one stop) darker than the highest white, which is as we would expect it to be, Zone VII—"textured brights." In the default Raw processing, using Photoshop, the highest white is about half a stop darker than it needs to be. However, raising the exposure by one stop shows how fragile these whites are—a serious loss of highlight detail, with clipping. However, if instead we raise the contrast in the Raw processor while leaving the exposure and brightness alone, we achieve in one stroke just the right white highlight and an expanded separation.

**Default**
*The default conversion of the color original.*

**Exposure raised**
*Exposure raised by one stop from the default.*

**Maximum contrast**
*Maximum contrast applied to the default black-and-white conversion.*

# DIGITAL ZONE SYSTEM

## DIGITAL ZONES

**The original, and converted into zones**
*The scene more or less as it appeared, with the most appropriate zone evaluation*

**1/125**
*Exposure at 1/125 sec (one f-stop less than the chosen setting)*

**1/60**
*Exposure at 1/60 sec (the chosen setting)*

**1/30**
*Exposure at 1/30 sec (one f-stop more than the chosen setting)*

**1/15**
*Exposure at 1/15 sec (2 f-stops more than the chosen setting)*

**1/8**
*Exposure at 1/8 sec (3 f-stops more than the chosen setting)*

CREATIVE CHOICES

**Using Lightzone 1**
*Rolling the cursor over the ZoneMapper to display similar tonal regions.*

**Using Lightzone 2**
*Dragging zones in the ZoneMapper to expand the dark areas.*

**The final version**

# HDR IN BLACK & WHITE

**High Dynamic Range photography (HDR) has rapidly achieved a popularity way beyond early expectations.**

The original techniques were invented as a means of capturing the full range of brightness in scenes containing deep shadow and the light source itself (for example, the sun). In the early days the use of HDR was confined to motion picture special effects, making what are called light probes. Now, however, HDR is another, powerful, processing tool in the photographer's armory. The results can be anything from naturalistic to surreal, and it is this range of possibility that attracts so many photographers. And, just as we saw on pages 58-61, black and white stands to benefit from HDR even more than color photography, simply because you can push the processing extremes further and still stay within the bounds of what looks photographic.

First, the basics. High Dynamic Range simply means a higher range of brightness than a normal camera can handle. Some people take a stricter definition, using HDR to refer to scenes which contain the main light source in view. In any case, we are talking about scenes that can be captured in their entirety only by taking a sequence of identical frames at different exposure settings, and then combining them. A high-end digital SLR has a dynamic range of around 11 stops, while an into-the-sun shot is more likely to have a range in excess of 20 stops.

In practical HDR photography there are three steps. First is capture, using a sequence of shots. Second is combining this sequence of images into a single HDR image file that contains all the brightness levels, more than can possibly be seen on a standard monitor or in a print. Step three is a software process of compressing all this information into a viewable form—in other words, an 8-bit image. This last step is the most demanding and most varied, and involves a software processing procedure called tonemapping. More on this in a moment, but interestingly, tonemapping can also be applied to regular, non-HDR image files, with equally interesting results.

## CAPTURE

Capturing a full range of brightness means keeping the camera ideally completely still, locked down on a tripod. Nevertheless, HDR creation software is nowadays good enough to be able to deal with slight movements between frames. But let's start with the classic capture procedure, in which nothing moves, neither camera, lens, nor objects in the scene. This lack of movement is important because merging the frames into one means achieving a perfect register.

The ideal spacing of exposure settings between frames is 2 stops. HDR software can handle this difference, so there is no advantage in shooting a smaller difference, such as 1 stop. However, most cameras that offer automatic bracketing go no higher than a 1-stop difference, so that unless you change the exposure settings manually, you will end up with more frames than you need. With the camera on a tripod, you might find that manual adjustment is a better choice, with less chance of camera shake if you shoot carefully. Mirror slap at slow shutter speeds is a prime cause of vibration, and locking the mirror of an SLR up is wise. The number of frames that you need to shoot in order to capture the full range depends on the scene, but you should aim for the following: the darkest exposure shows no highlight clipping—but only just—while the lightest exposure should have the darkest shadows as midtones. Provided that you use the camera's on-screen highlight clipping warning and the histogram, calculating the settings is easy. Remember, though, that the only adjustment to the exposure settings to make is to the shutter speed, not the aperture, because this will change depth of field and so interfere with registering the images later.

Begin with the darkest exposure. A couple of trial-and-error shots should get you to the exposure. Find the setting at which there is just a tiny amount of highlight clipping warning, then reduce by 1/3 or 1/2 stop from there. This sets one end-point of the sequence. For the second shot, open up by two stops on the shutter speed, such as for example from 1/500 sec to 1/125 sec. Do the same with each subsequent until the on-screen image looks almost completely over-exposed. For these later shots keep the histogram displayed on the camera's screen, and continue the sequence until the left-hand edge of the histogram is in the middle of the scale. If in doubt, over-shoot, as you can always delete frames later. One of the most common mistakes is not continuing the sequence far enough. You want the last frame to have no blacks whatsoever, and the darkest tones appear as midtones.

That is all there is to it. As mentioned, the HDR software that is discussed here—the software is the second step—has content-recognition algorithms that can usually cope with slight movements, and this is not just a safety net for minor knocks of the tripod, but it also makes it possible to shoot handheld—if you are careful and take some precautions to minimize movement. Without a tripod, use whatever surface and support you can find to help you brace. Use the camera's auto-bracketing, and set the shooting mode to the highest frame rate possible. There is also a different kind of movement that the software will attempt to deal with, and this is object movement in the scene, such as people walking or branches moving in the wind. This is more difficult to remove, but worth shooting for in any case.

**HDR theater**
*A fully processed shot of this theater creates a picture with detail to explore everywhere.*

# HDR IN BLACK & WHITE

## GENERATING THE HDR FILE

There are now several software applications that will accomplish HDR file merging, and each one has its particular method, but for simplicity we will stick to the two most popular, Photomatix and Photoshop. From the user's point of view, this is the simplest step in the operation and should need no intervention. Choosing the option to align images takes longer but is safer. If there was movement in the scene, and if the option is available, choose to remove it. Once the merging to HDR is complete, you will have a single file with 32 bits per channel instead of the usual 8 bits or 16 bits. It is, of course, impossible to view this range of detail on a normal 8-bit monitor, and will look unpleasantly contrasty, but this is irrelevant. In

Photomatix, a useful mini-viewer appears alongside the image that shows the full information visible from a tiny area under the cursor as you move it around. In Photoshop, a slider allows you to view the image lighter or darker (but this view has no effect on the actual image). A good step here is to save the image in one of the available HDR formats. For most purposes, it does not matter what you choose, but the most common is Radiance (.hdr), and the most economical in file size is Open EXR (.exr). It is not essential to save the HDR image, and you can instead proceed directly to the third step, tonemapping, but if you are likely to want to re-visit the HDR for an alternative tonemapping, you would then need to go through the HDR generation again. Saving the HDR can save time.

## TONE MAPPING

### Photomatix local
*Of the several HDR tonemapping software available, Photomatix is the most widely used, and its local tonemapping operator, called Details Enhancer, gives the strongest control. Even within this one application, however, there are many different effects, according to Strength, Luminosity and Light Smoothing in particular. The five distinct Light Smoothing settings have the greatest effect on the naturalism of the image; the setting chosen here gives excellent recovery of detail, contrast, and structure in the cloud and especially the shafts of lights spreading out from the top, though at the cost of some haloing.*

CREATIVE CHOICES

The most accurate HDR generation is, as you might expect, directly from Raw images, and this is always recommended. However, if you are aiming for a black-and-white HDR result, you are likely to find that you have more creative control if you convert the Raw images to monochrome before tonemapping. The alternative, going all the way through the process in color and then finally converting to black and white, is perfectly viable, but as we'll see, the creative choices during tonemapping are quite different between color and black and white. There are two ways of doing this. One is to convert the sequence of images from Raw to a black-and-white TIFF and then proceed. The other is to generate the HDR from Raw and then convert this to grayscale.

## TONEMAPPING

This is where all the work, and the fun, takes place. The algorithms, however, are complex and vary greatly from software to software. It helps to have some understanding of what goes on in tonemapping

in principle. This is the stage in the procedure in which the software attempts to squeeze the huge dynamic range in the image into a much smaller bit-depth so that it can actually be viewed in a normal way, on a screen or in a print. Simply compressing all the tones toward the middle equally will not produce a pleasing or realistic result. All of the useful tonemapping operators as the software is called (TMOs for short) employ a method to take into account the local neighborhoods in an image. For example, the extremely bright edges of a backlit cloud are likely to need a different scale of compression than do the shadows under a dark tree. Or, in one of the classic HDR situations, an interior with a view out through a window into bright sunlight, there will be two clearly demarcated areas—inside and outside—that need different compressions. The solution, mathematically complex, is called local tonemapping, and involves calculations that search around each pixel to see what tones its neighbors have.

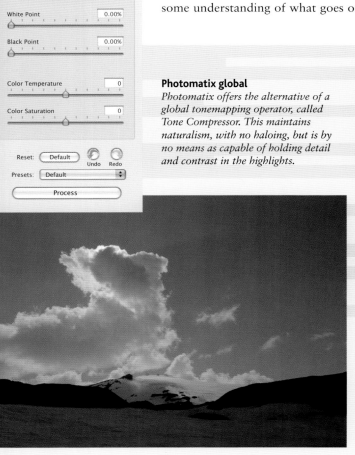

**Photomatix global**
*Photomatix offers the alternative of a global tonemapping operator, called Tone Compressor. This maintains naturalism, with no haloing, but is by no means as capable of holding detail and contrast in the highlights.*

**Photoshop local**
*Photoshop's principle tonemapper is called Local Adaptation, and in addition to Radius and Threshold controls, it allows mapping by means of a curve superimposed on a histogram. Control points on the curve can also be "locked" and made to behave like end-points—they are called Corners, and this allows sections of the curve to be manipulated independently.*

177

# HDR IN BLACK & WHITE

It's possible to spend a great deal of time and energy getting to grips with the details of tonemapping, but knowing more does not necessarily help in what is for most photographers a mainly creative process in experimenting with effect. Each tonemapping software has its own quirks and procedures, so familiarity with result is actually more useful than an understanding of the math involved, which can be very involved at any rate.

One of the characteristics of HDR tonemapping is a kind of halo around the border between strong contrasting tones, such as a roof-line against a bight sky. The width of the halo can usually be adjusted with the tonemapping controls, and making the width high is one way of reducing its appearance, Essentially, haloing is a failure of the software to recognize and deal with sharp tonal boundary edges, and from a purist point of view is a fault. However, from the point of

## INTO THE SUN CAPTURE SEQUENCE

1/2500 sec, ƒ16

1/1250 sec, ƒ16

1/640 sec, ƒ16

1/320 sec, ƒ16

view of creative interpretation, haloing can produce effects that many people like. The issue is contentious, but one of the interesting qualities of black and white is that it can absorb haloing better than can color in appearance. A broad halo is, after all, simply a tonal gradient, and with color removed from the equation this is by no means always objectionable—even to people for whom a halo is an artifact.

## INTO THE SUN

While HDR can be applied to any scene, only certain picture situations actually need this approach. The most demanding of all, with the highest dynamic range possible, is a shot that includes the major light source in the frame, and in which the light source needs to be fully captured, without clipping. In any outdoor scene, this means shooting into the sun. This image is one level down from that extreme, in that the sun is just behind the edge of a cloud.

Capture: Standard procedure for building a capture sequence for HDR is to begin with the darkest exposure, at which there is just no clipping, and increase the exposure by 2 stops for each subsequent frame, using the shutter speed only, until the final frame has the darkest shadows as midtones. Because this sequence was shot hand-held, the camera's auto bracketing was used, for which the maximum exposure gap between frames was one stop—more frames than necessary for HDR generation, but perfectly satisfactory. For a black-and-white HDR, these frames were converted to black and white before HDR generation.

**1/160 sec, ƒ16**

**1/80 sec, ƒ16**

**1/40 sec, ƒ16**

# HDR IN BLACK & WHITE

## INTERPRETATION

Tonemapping can be as much about skill, taste, and style as technicalities. With so many adjustable tools, and many quite different algorithms invented by software developers, there is no such thing as a standard procedure. In particular, each image has its own characteristics, and even experienced HDR users are unlikely to be able to predict exactly which settings will produce a desired result. Tonemapping calls for experiment. In this example of a church interior (which is one of the classic HDR picture situations), two versions out of many show the contrast between an approach geared to revealing detail and an approach aimed at reproducing atmosphere (which includes the glow—actually flare—from the spotlighting).

## CAPTURE SEQUENCE

On a tripod, spaced 2 stops apart.

**1/2 sec, ƒ22**

**2 sec, ƒ22**

**8 sec, ƒ22**

**30 sec, ƒ22**

**Version 1**
*Concentrates on recovery of detail.*

**Version 2**
*This version balances detail with a more photographic, flare-and-shadow feeling.*

# TONEMAPPING WITHOUT HDR

**The tonemapping procedures that are so necessary when shooting HDR can also be applied to ordinary, non-HDR images, and we can treat it as its own form of post-processing.**

In fact, tonemapping in one form or another has crept in to most processing software suites, although it is not always identified as such. The value is that it offers a different kind of control for recovering detail and for adjusting contrast in local areas of brightness or shadow. Just how these effects compare with the more traditional curve-based techniques deserves experimentation, not least because aggressive use of tonemapping produces artificial-looking images that may seem to lack traditional "photographic" qualities.

Probably the most-used tonemapping method is Photoshop's Shadows/Highlights adjustment. This is radius-based and allows lightening and contrast control of shadows, darkening and contrast control of highlights, together with contrast adjustment of the midtones in between these two zones. While I have no intention of giving a tutorial on this method here (there are other sources for that), it is worth promoting an exploration of what it can do as part of the processing workflow. We already showed something of this earlier in "Your processing workflow" (pages 90-93) and in "Basic processing" (pages 96-103).

But there are also ways of using HDR tonemapping. As these are designed to work on 32-bit HDR formatted files, the starting point is to convert your 16-bit TIFF to 32-bit and then save it in one of the HDR formats, such as Radiance or OpenEXR. In fact, if you stay within Photoshop, simply the conversion to 32-bit gives you access to the Photoshop tonemapping algorithms when you return to 16-bit mode. The example here uses a TIFF converted in Photoshop to OpenEXR and then tonemapped in Photomatix, the leading HDR software.

**Original scan**
*The original, a scan from a transparency.*

| SHADOWS/HIGHLIGHTS | |
| --- | --- |
| **SHADOWS** | |
| AMOUNT | 8% |
| TONAL WIDTH | 76% |
| RADIUS | 54px |
| **HIGHLIGHTS** | |
| AMOUNT | 35% |
| TONAL WIDTH | 7% |
| RADIUS | 30px |
| **ADJUSTMENTS** | |
| COLOR CORRECTION | +20 |
| MIDTONE CONTRAST | +52 |
| BLACK CLIP | 0.01% |
| WHITE CLIP | 0.01% |

**1.** Strength of lightening, here modest

**2.** 30% tonal width extends lightening to this shade of gray

**3.** High radius because shadow areas are extensive

**4.** Strength of darkening, here just a little, otherwise highlights would be flat

**5.** Width covers just torso tones

**6.** Lower radius for highlights as their extent is less than that of shadows

**7.** No color correction needed for monochrome

**8.** A slight amount of increased contrast to the middle grays

**Shadow highlight tool's targets**
*The annotations show which of the many Shadows/Highlights sliders were considered important for handling this image. There are no standard recommendations for this adjustment method, and each image has its own peculiarities and ways of responding. This makes it not only legitimate, but essential to play with the sliders to gauge the look.*

### Targeted tone enhancement
*Tonal enhancement of the image shown on page 46, emphasizing structural detail in the clouds, and so radically altering the focus of attention.*

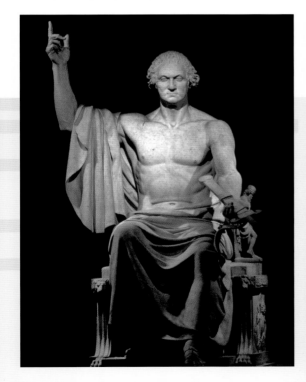

### The final image
*With shadows opened, torso highlights moderated and a slight overall increase of contrast in the midtones in between. The base shadow background has been kept rich.*

### Standard conversion
*"Normal" processing of a photograph taken in a ruined Khmer temple, Banteay Chhmar, without post-processing.*

### Details enhancer
*Using Photomatix, and the settings shown here for its local tonemapping operator, called Details Enhancer, a quite different look is created, less "photographic" and with more local detail visible.*

# ADDING TINTS

For the purpose of adding a tint, toning was generally used according to how the printer (very frequently the printer was also the photographer) felt the image would respond. Sepia, selenium, gold, and platinum toners were the most widely used. Each worked by replacing the metallic silver in the print (which gave black) with another compound or metal. Sepia toning uses a sulphide compound, selenium converts silver to silver selenide, with a red-brown to purple-brown effect depending on the strength, platinum and gold are metal replacements, with gold giving a blue-black tint.

All of these are easily reproduced digitally, either by manipulating the curves, or by taking advantage of the presets that several processing applications offer, as shown here. A further development is split-toning, which chemically could be the result of a wide range of processes, including imperfect fixing. Typically, contrasting tints, such as yellowish against bluish, are present in the same image, most usually split according to density. Thus, the shadow areas can be one tint, the highlights another. Again, this can be done digitally using curves or by making alternate highlight and shadow selections, or by using split-toning sliders in some processing software.

**From very early in the history of photography, it was realized that bathing the developed print in certain chemical solutions could do two things: improve the stability of the image and/or add a colored tint.**

**LightZone**
*In LightZone, applying a black-and-white preset and adding a yellow tone.*

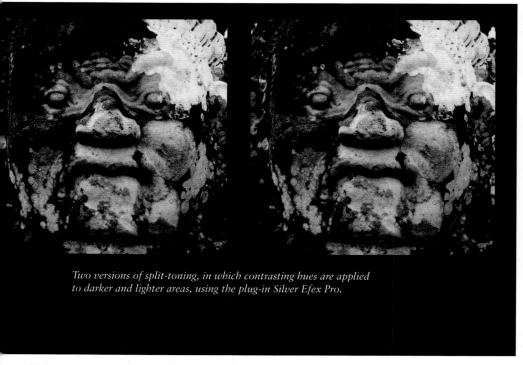

*Two versions of split-toning, in which contrasting hues are applied to darker and lighter areas, using the plug-in Silver Efex Pro.*

# LIGHTZONE STYLES

In common with many editing programs, LightZone offers a number of "Styles," including toning presets. Here are some examples.

**Brown Yellow**

**Golden Brick**

**Golden Sepia**

**Palladium**

**Palladium Gold**

**Palladium Silver**

# OLD PROCESS EFFECTS

**N**ow more than ever there are revivals of old photographic processes—or at least in their visual effect. While the goal of most digital photographic technology is perfection of image quality, processes like the Cyanotype and the Calotype offer atmospheric qualities that for some photographers have more resonance.

The whole question of simulation is a disputed one. The objections tend to fall into two camps: one, that simply approximating an effect by digital manipulation is false, and two, that it veers toward pictorialism, which for a large part of the American history of photography was despised.

These are both, however, matters of judgment, and I don't intend to pass mine here. The argument FOR simulating old processes is that these historical techniques threw up styles of imagery that were interesting in themselves, and that now digitally we have the opportunity to learn what caused them and to re-create them. In other words, the visual result rather than the process.

Processing software and plug-ins have preset effects, and applications such as LightRoom, LightZone, SilverEfex Pro, and Alien Skin Exposure 2, among others, have between them a good selection of these old effects. These are displayed here.

**One of the services that digital photography and broadband sharing has performed has been to stimulate interest in *all* aspects of photography.**

**Antique Plate,**
*Featuring fading, vignetting, and discoloration.*

Cyanotype

Ferrotype (tintype)

Ambrotype

Solarization

187

# SECTION 4
# PRINTING & DISPLAY

Black-and-white photography's rich and long tradition has, until very recently, been expressed at its highest level in the form of the fine print, hanging in a gallery. It was, of course, widely presented in magazines, books and newspapers, but offset reproduction like this was always seen as a kind of pale imitation of the real thing. This was in contrast to color photography, where the fine print was a minority because of the technical problems in controlling the printed image, and color images were much more easily reproduced in magazines and books. A black-and-white negative never carried a final image, just the means for making one when printed, and this established printing as an essential part of the artistic process as well as of the technical.

Digital photography and reproduction has changed all of this. On the one hand, desktop digital printing has come of age, with printer and paper manufacturers fully acknowledging the importance of black and white. On the other hand online, on-screen display is a new medium that suits black and white just as well as it does color. Ansel Adams foresaw this as long ago as the 1970s, when he said in interview, "...you will see perfectly beautiful images on a screen. I'd say that would be very handsome. They would be almost as close as the best reproductions. That's a very important thing. I could like video [he was imagining this in terms of the possibilities foreseeable then], using maybe two cameras, to say all the things I've wanted to say for years." And a newly accessible form of display and presentation is the limited edition book. Formerly, a black-and-white monograph was affordable only if the publisher felt that it would have healthy retail sales through bookshops. Now, however, a growing number of companies offer on-line book publishing services, with editions as low as one!

# LEARNING FROM MASTER PRINTERS

There are two strands to this. One is the understandable need to at least match, and ideally surpass, the print qualities that can be extracted from gelatin silver. The other is using gelatin silver printing as a craft resource, not in technique but in its aims and in the creative judgment that traditional printers acquired.

The major difference between the two processes is in fact the sequence, because while the adjustments in gelatin silver printing are made on the spot, during enlargement and in the developing bath—very much a personal "performance"—in digital printing most of the preparation is before the image is sent to the printer. Nevertheless, if we're looking at the creative decisions, how and why these are made are more important than at what stage. On the following pages we look at contrasting approaches to producing what Ansel Adams liked to call an "expressive" print. Being black-and-white imagery, all of this lends itself extremely well to distinctions in tonality and to some extremes of darkness and brightness. Nevertheless, the underlying thought processes of these creative decisions can be transferred to a color palette, as we will see.

**It's a valid question to ask how much we can learn from the long craft history of gelatin silver printing, provided that we appreciate how different this is technically from modern digital printing.**

## BASIC WORKFLOW IN GELATIN SILVER PRINTING

Choose paper grade

Choose developer

Crop

Dodge and burning

Choosing developer

Controlling development time and temperature, including selective development

Spotting and etching

Reducing and toning more than light ones.

## BASIC WORKFLOW IN DIGITAL PRINTING

Prepare image to its on-screen appearance

Choose paper and profile

Make fine adjustments

Print

**Working In My Darkroom**
*Ansel Adams self-portrait, 1936.*
*©Ansel Adams Publishing Rights Trust / Corbis*

# LEARNING FROM
# MASTER PRINTERS

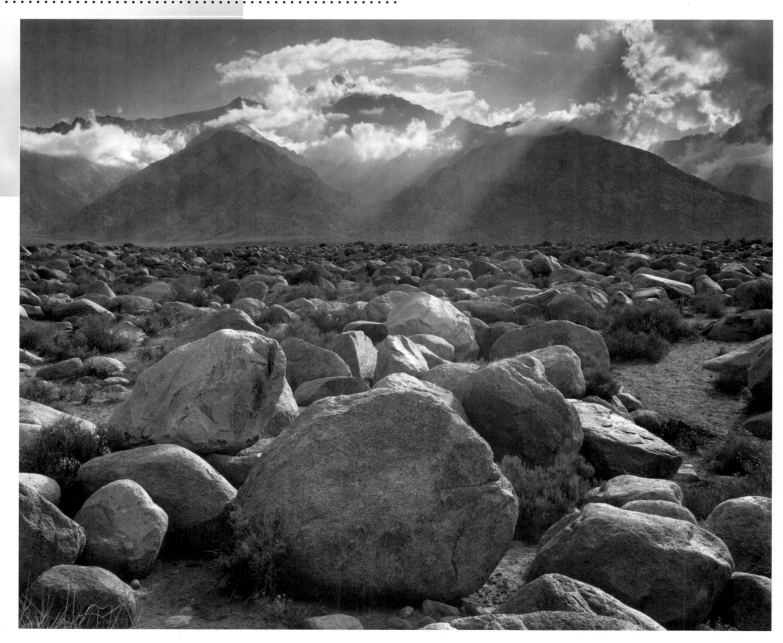

**Mt Williamson, Sierra
Nevada, from Manzanar,
California, 1949**
*By Ansel Adams.
©Ansel Adams Publishing
Rights Trust / Corbis*

PRINTING & DISPLAY

Ansel Adams' approach to printing is among the most valuable to learn, because of three things: his consummate skill, his fairly traditional and mainstream views on what a good print should look like, and the fact that he wrote, a great deal, about all of this. In other words, there is an art to deciding how your image should print, and it was essential not to do it in a formulaic way.

"A fine print has been generally assumed to have a full range of values, clear delineation of form and texture, and a satisfactory print 'color.' But what a catastrophe it would be if all photographs only met these criteria!" Time and again, in his notes on specific images, he comes back to the mood of the occasion, how a particular landscape (most of his images were landscapes) affected him at the time. For example, "The mood of the scene was dramatic and called for a deep-valued image—a literal rendition of values would not do at all!" And "Although the scene was of low general contrast, my visualization of the final print was quite vigorous. The subject had a very dramatic potential." And "Printing this picture is not easy, because the mood is so important to hold. Clearly the white church should dominate, yet it must not be harsh or lacking in texture."

Until 1937, when the material became difficult to find, Strand made most of his prints on platinum paper, which was renowned for its long gray scale, and it was this distinctive quality that Strand responded to. Even so, platinum prints as normally developed tend to lack the density of black that most photographs require, so Strand added extra platinum emulsion and followed through with gold-toning to extend the tonal range down into the blacks.

Yet Strand was not in thrall to any formula. In a 1946 seminar, he said, "I have been very conscious in the past twenty years that it is very easy to standardize photography. It is easy to find a paper that you like and you make all your prints on that paper," going on to explain that while platinum, with its "much greater scale than bromide" was ideal for his images of the American Southwest, "a land of plenteous sunshine, and the general tone and feel of the country is warm and rich," for his pictures in northeastern Canada "it was the wrong paper. The north is cold, the color that best showed this was something with a black overtone."

Bill Brandt, as we saw at the beginning of the book, changed the way he interpreted his negatives over the years. There are examples of negatives revisited at a later date and printed much more harshly and darker, to the point where many of the shadow areas are completely blocked up. This drift to darkness, which sometimes led to daylit scenes being transformed into dusk or night images, was accompanied by increasing contrast, and from the middle of the 1950s he began choosing harder and harder grades of paper. "Soot and chalk" is probably a crude way of putting it, but the gradual elimination of middle tones from Brandt's prints gave them a very distinctive look. Needless to say, Brandt believed in the photographer having full control over the entire process "I consider it essential that the photographer should do his own printing and enlarging. The final effect of the finished print depends so much on these operations. And only the photographer himself knows the effect he wants." As he also noted, "It takes a long time to produce a good print."

Don McCullin, as we also saw, also prints his own photographs. "I lay it on a bit thick, I know I do, but I really like working with angry clouds, and naked trees, and English hedgerows and things." He also now adds more contrast, saying, "so that the thing really comes at you—a kind of hit and run," although not to the extremes of Brandt.

# CONTROL AT ALL COSTS: W. EUGENE SMITH

Even Bill Brandt did this when it suited him—in his famous print of the moorland house that was the scene for Wuthering Heights, he used a second negative for the sky, an act that appalled the artist David Hockney who had purchased a print (this and other instances recorded by Nigel Warburton). Brandt in fact argued, "Photography is not a sport...I believe there are no rules in photography.

**In opposition to the school of printing thought that holds the print to be a more-or-less faithful rendition of what the photographer saw, a number of photographer-printers have used the darkroom as the scene for creating images that are startlingly different in mood and tone from what was shot. In some cases, even the content was manipulated, chiefly through including parts of other negatives.**

A photographer is allowed to do anything, anything, in order to improve his picture."

The American documentary photographer W. Eugene Smith, 1918-1978, is an even more consistent example of someone who believed that art had priority over objective reality. Moreover, his skill at printing allowed him to achieve remarkable results in his darkroom marathons. In his picture essay for *Life* on a psychiatric hospital in Haiti, extreme burning-in created images with a strange intensity of lighting focused on faces and eyes. In other instances he simply improved the composition by inserting parts of images from other negatives, all under the enlarger. His view, quoted by biographer Jim Hughes, was: "This is the way I see it. This is the way I feel it, and I think this is perfectly legitimate in that photography has very little of reality in it, and then only on the lower level of simple recognition. Beyond that, in transmission of the inner feeling, I feel that everything that is honest to the situation is honest to the photograph."

As one of the contributors to Smith's 1998 photographic biography *W. Eugene Smith: The Camera As Conscience* wrote, "Digital manipulation, perhaps Photoshop, would have been Smith's addiction today." It's hard to argue with.

Eugene Smi
©*Corbis*

# DIGITAL PRINTING

One thing I am not going to do here is discuss the finer points of the techniques and technology behind digital printing, for which there are many sources of information (and not unexpectedly I suggest *The Art of Digital Printing on Your Epson Printer*, which I co-wrote). Rather, I want to look at the more fundamental decisions of paper, ink, tone, and the subtle distinctions between inkjet and silver bromide. Archival arguments still erupt occasionally, but with forecasts now in the 200 year-plus range for some inks, this is fast becoming a non-issue.

**Black and white has long held the strongest position in fine art photography (you need look no further than the catalog of any major photography auction), and the fine art print is for most people the ideal end-product.**

Silver bromide printing is continuous tone, and while ink-jet printing is not (the head sprays a pattern of extremely fine dots), with a modern high-quality machine the results can be indistinguishable. Nevertheless, silver prints have their own look and feel. In recent years, a number of paper manufacturers have aimed for products that will match the specific look of air-dried fibre-based glossy paper, and if used with the appropriate inks, they are a close match. But one of the things that ink-jet paper excels at is matt printing. Papers such as Hahnemulle's Photo Rag have helped to raise matte prints to a much higher level of acceptance than in silver-print days, and ink improvements from companies like Epson have helped to solve the Dmax issue. A high Dmax, or the maximum black density, has always been sought after. One reason why glossy prints have held such a strong position in fine art photography is that they improve the apparent Dmax. I say "apparent" because a glossy surface works as the viewer sees the print from different angles, at some positions reflecting dark surfaces. It is worth holding a glossy print and moving it slightly to appreciate how this works.

There are varieties of and preferences for inksets, including black-only—too many to go into here. At the time of writing, Epson hold the premier position for printers, and their solution for black-and-white printing is therefore probably the most widely used. This consists of three black inks (Black, Light Black, and Light Light Black) in addition to five color inks, of which the first can be swapped between Photo Black (for glossy and semi-matte papers) and Matte Black (for matte papers).

The printer driver is critical, and until recently the driver supplied with the machine, even from Epson, offered less control and consistency than RIP software. RIP (Raster Image Processing) chooses the ink combination and amount in a more sophisticated way, but the software is quite costly. The latest drivers, however, are challenging this supremacy. One issue with black and white is that the black inks are carbon based, and carbon has a certain brownish cast. This can be compensated for by the addition of tiny amounts of color ink during printing. One problem with this, slowly being brought under control as the technology develops, is metamerism, in which a black-and-white print can take on a different color cast under different light source.

Above all, and we've dealt with this already in Chapter 2, digital printing allows all the image preparation to be done beforehand. No longer do dodging, burning, and other controls depend on the performance skills of the printer (now the name of a machine, at any rate). This should mean much finer control and absolute consistency of reproduction, but at the same time (and this may matter for some collectors) less individuality of each print.

# PRINTING QUALITY CHECKLIST

Calibrate (i.e. profile) the printer for the specific paper and inkset.

Calibrate the monitor.

Choose the appropriate printer driver or RIP software.

Take advantage of black-and-white settings in the driver or RIP, if available, particularly with regard to controlling metamerism.

Match ink to paper, if this is possible and/or necessary (e.g. Matte Black to a matte paper).

Check and maintain print-head cleanliness.

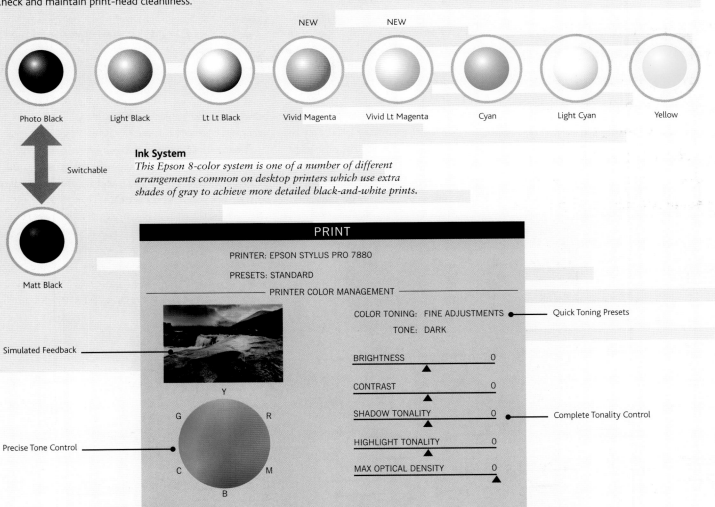

NEW                NEW

| Photo Black | Light Black | Lt Lt Black | Vivid Magenta | Vivid Lt Magenta | Cyan | Light Cyan | Yellow |

Switchable

Matt Black

**Ink System**
*This Epson 8-color system is one of a number of different arrangements common on desktop printers which use extra shades of gray to achieve more detailed black-and-white prints.*

## PRINT

PRINTER: EPSON STYLUS PRO 7880

PRESETS: STANDARD

——— PRINTER COLOR MANAGEMENT ———

Simulated Feedback

COLOR TONING: FINE ADJUSTMENTS ●——— Quick Toning Presets

TONE: DARK

BRIGHTNESS          0
▲

CONTRAST            0
▲

SHADOW TONALITY     0          ●——— Complete Tonality Control
▲

HIGHLIGHT TONALITY  0
▲

MAX OPTICAL DENSITY 0
▲

Y

G       R

Precise Tone Control

C       M

B

HORIZONTAL: 0

VERTICAL:   0

# MOUNTING & FRAMING

The choices for print display are huge, and go well beyond the traditional wood frame. As photographic shows in galleries and museums become more popular, there has been an increase in experiment with ways of mounting prints. Display is also subject to fashion, and of particular note is the trend toward large prints and the trend toward flush-mounting on metal and other non-traditional substrates. One of the best pieces of research you can do is to visit city photo galleries and compare how they choose to display their collections. Some of the mounting methods described here are not archival, which though important for prints being sold, may not matter at all if you simply intend to display them and are prepared to run off another print in the event of discoloration. Face-mounting and mounting on aluminium, both currently fashionable, may be archival, but of course the print is permanently bonded to the substrate. This, however, seems to be accepted by most buyers.

The mounting alternatives shown in close-up on these pages are from Imagey, a supplier in the UK (http://www.imagey.co.uk/), and DryTac (www.drytac.com or www.hotpress.co.uk).

**The choices for print display are huge, and go well beyond the traditional wood frame.**

## TRADITIONAL FRAMES

The traditional method of mounting and framing is a frame with mitred corners, holding a matte. Mattes are normally archival board into which is cut a window with a 45-degree sloping inner edge, and this is a specialized process, needing either great skill with a blade, or a mat-cutter. Typical materials for the frame are wood (natural, stained, painted) with popular woods being maple, walnut, mahogany, oak; and aluminum (anodized, stainless, black)

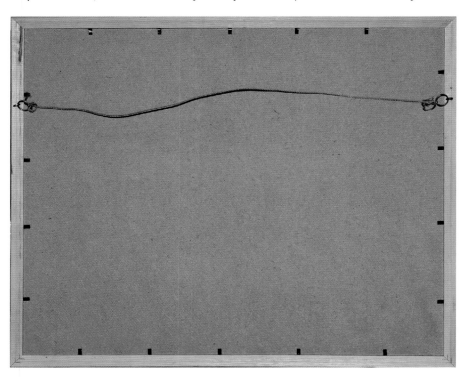

**Back**
*The back of a traditional frame with a wire for hanging to a hook.*

**Traditional frames**
*These frames have a classic
look that works in almost
any environment*

## BLOCK MOUNTS
## (MDF, FOAMEX, ACRYLIC)

Block mounted prints are on relatively thick panels,
typically 4 to 6 inches (10 to 15mm). The two most
usual substrates, non-archival, are MDF and Foamcore.
The latter is much lighter than MDF, and so more
suitable for large prints. Acrylic is another option.

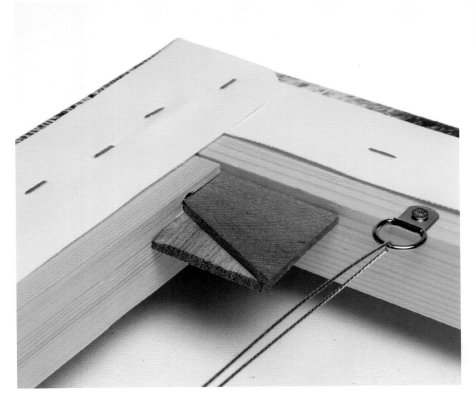

## CANVAS WRAPS

In this, the image is ink-jet printed directly on to canvas.
The canvas is then hand-stretched over a wooden
stretcher complete with corner wedges to maintain a
taut finish, as shown to the left. On the canvas print
side of the stretcher the frame typically has a rounded
lip to prevent show through from the front.

MOUNTING & FRAMING

# MOUNTING & FRAMING

## ALUMINUM MOUNT

The back of the print is bonded to an aluminum substrate with a honeycomb core and a silicon base supple sealant (again, there are non-archival sealants, so it is important to use a non-corrosive version) This is usually undertaken by specialist mounters, as achieving a perfectly flat bond, with no bubbles or particles, is difficult. For larger mounts, a honeycomb panel, essentially two aluminum skins sandwiching a honeycomb, offers rigidity while maintaining a low weight, though at some cost.

## ACRYLIC SANDWICH

Avoiding the use of an adhesive for face-mounting, a similar effect is possible by sandwiching the print between two acrylic panels and securing the sandwich with fixing studs at the corners.

## ACRYLIC FLOATS

These are clear acrylic box frames with a solid recessed, typically wooden, frame. In the standard version the print is sandwiched between subframe and the acrylic frame with no gap. In an "air-gap" float there is a deeper recess that allows a gap between print and the acrylic box frame front. The photographic print is dry-mounted to the backing subframe.

## ACRYLIC FACE-MOUNT

Front-mounting, also known as face-mounting, is a process that involves bonding the face of the print to a clear acrylic sheet, using an optically clear adhesive. Behind the print is another substrate, so that the print is sandwiched between two sheets. Not all optically clear adhesives are archival, and in any case great care and skill is necessary to avoid trapping bubbles or particles. A typical combination of substrates would be 1/8-inch (3mm) Plexigas for the front mount and 1/4-inch (6mm) black Sintra for the back mount. Alternatives for the back mount include Dibond, Gatorboard, and Plexiglas.

# HANGING & LIGHTING PRINTS

H anging and lighting (the two go hand in hand) are by no means obvious procedures, and demand thought and judgment. For this reason, I'm spending more time on this than on printing itself, about which there is endless instruction available, much of it in the printer manuals themselves.

A trawl through the internet for advice on hanging prints catches a succession of "rules" about hanging. Well-meaning though these may be, they have much the same predictability as rules of composition. The comparison is more than useful, because hanging prints on a wall is indeed composition, and so subject to all the variables you might expect. In fact, the best single piece of advice I can give is to plan the hanging as preparation for taking a photograph of the room and installation. The variables are the size of the print, the size of the wall space, the room and its furnishings, the number of prints that you intend to hang together, your personal taste, and of course, the subject and general character of each of the images.

**Considering that the display of the finished mounted image is the final and crucial stage of making photographs for prints, it is woefully under-reported.**

There is also the matter of choice. It's usual to be in the position of having a limited number of spaces available in the home, and certain images that you particularly want to display. Matching the one to the other is more than likely to involve a compromise, and may not be perfect.

Lighting prints is inextricable from planning where to hang them, and if hanging receives little attention in the literature on photography, lighting comes close to the point of being ignored. And yet, it is immensely important. First, prints deserve to be lit prominently, so that they stand out relatively on the wall. Second, the angle and concentration of the light needs to be such that reflections do not interfere with viewing, and this is by no means always easy to set up. Gallery conditions are usually easier to control because there is usually nothing else going on in the space, and all the lighting effort can be concentrated on the prints. In a home, the normal ambience has to be considered too, and prints rarely have top priority then.

Unwanted reflections are a major issue, exacerbated by a glossy print surface (very common in black and white in order to deepen the appearance of blacks) and by a transparent covering if there is one (glass or

**Working together**
*Below The four frames here each contain part of a greater whole picture.*

**Corridor**
*BELOW LEFT This corridor has been adapted as a hanging space with wood panels.*

**Tall wall**
*ABOVE A high ceiling is the perfect spot for a large canvas print.*

**Consistency**
*Though the pictures are grouped, the frame style is the same throughout.*

acrylic). There are two basic alternatives: spotlighting or diffuse overhead lighting. Spotlighting can be very efficient because it can be concentrated on the print alone, but the key is the angle between its beam and the viewing angle. A small angle (with the spot close to the viewing axis, near the viewer) causes reflections. A high ceiling is ideal, as placing spots there—on a track if there are several prints—widens the angle. The tightness of the beam angle also needs to be considered, and it must at least cover the print area. Shown here is what I consider the absolute ideal for spotlighting—a shaped focusing spot. This is the most meticulous kind of lighting possible for prints, and very few galleries even attempt it. The advantages, however, are great.

An alternative is to take advantage of any skylights that the space may have. As in still-life product lighting, a diffuse area light from overhead has the advantage of bathing the entire wall with a soft light, minimizing hotspot reflections and automatically giving a broad even illumination to the print. However, as night falls, the effect is lost, unless, as in the conservatory example shown here, you add an artificial light high overhead to take over from daylight.

The color of the light—in particular the color temperature—may not be as important for black-and-white prints as for color (less metamerism), but it still applies to an extent, as you need to maintain at least the impression of neutral grays. Fortunately, the human vision system (HVS) adapts well to changes in color temperature, so that as long as there is one dominant type of illumination (such as daylight or tungsten), this will largely take care of itself. Compact fluorescent lights (CFLs) are as unpleasant for black-and-white prints as for anything else, but unfortunately seem to be taking over, and at least they are easier on the eye than they are on the camera sensor.

# HANGING & LIGHTING PRINTS

The following are certainly not rules, but I hope more than simply tips; they are principles to consider, and they are based on more universal ideas of composing photographs (my book *The Photographer's Eye* has much more on this).

## VIEWING HEIGHT

The most comfortable viewing height for a print is when the center is at eye level. Of course, people's height varies, but for a print intended to be viewed while standing, which is normal, about 60 inches (1.5m) from the center of the image to the floor is typical.

## VISUAL WEIGHT

At normal, first-sight distance (not necessarily the same thing as the distance a viewer may approach for detailed inspection), consider the "visual weight" of the mounted print. For example, this will be very different between a low-key image dominated by rich, dark tones, and a high-key photograph with a few small elements against a largely white ground. The first will have a strong visual weight, the latter fairly weak.

**Balance**
*The low but solid Japanese cupboard was moved left to balance the large black-and-white landscape. Note also that the bonsai tree "points" toward the print, so introducing an extra dynamic element to the composition.*

PRINTING & DISPLAY

# TARGETED LIGHTING

Spot lights that carefully project light directly onto the photograph's area, and ignore the surrounding wall, help bring a picture to life by seeming to extend the dynamic range. The frames and lens restrict the light so it is projected precisely.

**Targeted spot**

**Frames for targeted spots**

**Unlit picture**

**Light on, picture removed**

**Picture with targeted spot on light**

### COMFORTABLE VIEWING DISTANCE

The most comfortable viewing distance for any image is one at which the image can more-or-less be taken in at once. Given the way that the eye and brain work, flicking rapidly across a scene, there is no definite measure for this, but an angle of view of about 40° takes in an entire frame, making the viewing distance for a 8 × 10-inch (20 × 25cm) print about 30 inches (75cm). One role of thumb is a viewing distance of two-and-a-half times the print diagonal. Having said this, there is nothing to say that this is necessary. For example, the power of a very large print often comes from the fact that it exceeds the field of view, in much the same way that an IMAX screen draws its audience right into the action. And the subject of the image can vary hugely in whether it reads at a glance or whether it demands close inspection.

### TWO VIEWING DISTANCES

Smaller prints have two viewing distances, as suggested above. The first is in the context of the entire room; they punctuate the wall space and act as elements in the overall design. The second is much closer, when someone approaches to look at them individually.

### GROUP FUNCTIONS AS ONE

A group of smaller prints, if spaced fairly closely, functions at first glance as a single unit, and can be treated as such when planning your space.

### SPACING

While it is normal to keep constant spacing between prints in a group, different sizes may suggest different spacing. Close spacing unifies the group, making them function more as one; looser spacing gives each more individuality. There is no better or worse here.

### PATTERN OF GROUPING

Experiment with spacing and the pattern of a group, and do not feel compelled to keep them all in a straight line, or symmetrical, or indeed otherwise! A useful method is to photograph the space, make a print, and then cut out small prints to scale of the images you intend to hang, and move them around on the print, as shown here.

## DIRECTIONAL

Directed halogen lights have a project fairly small area of bright light when targeted towards a wall. This is a great spot to hang an image, though the fall-off means the light will never be completely even.

1. Decide whether to hang from one point or two.

2. Fix the wire at the back of the frame.

3. Lift the wire at full tension and measure the distance from this high point to the top of the frame.

4. Calculate half the height of the frame (that is, to the mid-point).

5. From the floor, measure upwards 60 inches (or whatever viewing height you have decided on), mark lightly on the wall with a pencil .

6. Upwards from this, measure and mark half the height of the frame (as in step 4).

7. Downward from this second mark, measure the distance from step 3.

8. Place nail(s) or hanger(s) at this point.

## GALLERY HANGING
This is usually quite different from hanging in available spaces in a home, and the lighting in any good gallery space is made for the job. Ceiling spots are the most common. Spacing is usually much wider, in order to isolate individual prints and give them sufficient viewing space.

## LIGHT TO HEIGHTEN RELATIVE BRIGHTNESS
The basic principle of most lighting is to make the print stand out clearly, and this usually means from its surroundings. See the examples here, particularly the shaped focusing spot.

## AVOID LIGHTING HOTSPOTS
Just as if you were photographing a piece of flat artwork, keep the beams from spotlights at the maximum angle to the on-axis viewing direction, in order to minimize reflections from the print surface.

Consider both daylight and night-time lighting if you use daylight to illuminate a print: consider what you might do to substitute for this with artificial lighting during the evening.

## WHITE WALLS
While you can overrule this on matters of personal preference, a plain white wall is the classic background, and very hard to beat for simplicity and presentation. Colored walls do very badly for most photographic prints, including black and white.

# A CUSTOMIZED SOLUTION

The project was to create a comprehensive portrait of the client and his third-generation cattle ranch in Australia—a narrative memento that would range over his life and favorite things, and that would continue to interest and surprise. It was shot in a number of sessions over the course of a year.

Callister wanted a form of mounting that would combine the many images but would also integrate them. She decided to create a piece that would be seen at one viewing yet contain many different stories and individual stand-alone pieces, and to this end printed each photograph as a miniature, while her husband hand-crafted the small individual wooden blocks. What initially started as an installation of 50 pieces eventually became a tableau of 210 pieces, and the beauty of it lies in the fact that it is both a work of grand scale yet intimate. Each piece is independent and can be taken down, handled, and savored individually. Moreover, as each has its own hook, the entire tableau can be re-arranged to change the narrative, or to create smaller stories within.

**In a perfect example of thinking imaginatively when it comes to mounting, photographer Sue Callister and her husband Alberto Saro invented this "tableau" system, as they call it, for a portrait commission in black and white.**

Archival dry mounting tissue and 4-ply archival mounting board are cut to size. The tissue is tacked onto the photograph and then onto the board. They are carefully placed into the hot press to activate the tissue and then left to cure and are stored. The photographs are then mounted using archival adhesives onto the blocks.

**Frames**
*ALL ON THIS PAGE Each individual print is made at exactly the same size and mounted onto an identical wooden frame.*

**The whole**
*LEFT AND BELOW The arrangement of prints is as much an artwork as each individual photograph.*

# LIMITED EDITION BOOKS

The expense of publishing with a normal book run, however, restricted this to a few professionals—after all, sales of at least a few thousand copies were needed to justify the operation financially. Now, however, production and printing techniques have lowered the entry barrier drastically. Inconceivable until a few years ago, a number of companies have sprung up, dealing through the internet, to print as few copies of your own, self-designed book as you want, and at a price that is affordable. Here, to demonstrate the process, I'm showing the procedure for one of the high-end publishers, AsukaBook, who deal exclusively with professional photographers. These books—you might want an edition of just 100, for example—clearly have many uses, such as creating a promotional edition for a corporate client, or a wedding book. Here, we're showcasing the production of a fine-art black-and-white coffee table book.

**In many ways, the ultimate show for many photographers is a book, printed to fine art standards.**

Type of Book: Book Bound
Type of Cover: Hard Cover
Book Case: Frosted Case
Cover Option:
Book Size: 11 x 8
Number of Sides:
Page Finish: Varnish
Hot Stamp Text:
Color Profile: Adobe RGB
Client Reference : MF_DM

Book Bound

Hard Cover

Varnish

☑ Display and print the file name below each image.   Font

**AuskaBook**
*AuskaBook provide design software to assist making layouts.*

Book Bound Hard Cover  11x8 10P

Large

Please select layout template

# LIMITED EDITION
# BOOKS

**Layout in progress**
*The wraparound jacket in the layout software.*

**Bound cover**
*The final product.*

**Sipcase**
*The book slides into a
frosted plastic slipcase.*

**Gutter precaution**
*An interior double page
spread. Bookbinding
inevitably creates a
gutter in the center,
which loses some of the
image. It's important to
avoid a layout in which
a key element, such as
an eye, would disappear
into this.*

# BLACK & WHITE ON YOUR OWN SITE

There are now so many options available for any individual to display photographs that it is possible to set up a personal presence on the web within minutes, and most photographers already have. The easiest of all are photo-sharing sites such as Flickr, but for the most control, particularly over the appearance of each web page, having your own dedicated website is the logical step. I'll assume at this point that you either have or know how to create a website, and get straight to the important issue of how to make black-and-white photographs look their best on it. If you do not know how to create a site you can easily find and contact local designers, or buy pre-built sites to tailor to your needs, on the web.

**The web is now the major display site for photography, and for speed and reach it cannot be bettered.**

## WEBSITE TIPS

Before all else, it is important to have a clear idea of exactly what you want from your site. Here I took advice from the creative director of a leading London design agency with great experience in web design, Susanna Cook. She gave the following advice:

**1. What's the purpose of your site?**
First decide what you want from your website. Are you trying to display your best images? Share them with friends? Offer them for sale?

**2. Be proud of your images.**
Maintain confidence in the excellence of your images, and treat the pages as a presentation of fine photography.

**3. The image takes top priority.**
The first priority should be displaying the images. That means large and/or dominant on the screen, with a fitting rather than competing background.

**4. Do you want to conform or be different?**
Do you want your site to fit in with the general standards and style of similar photography sites? Or do you want to stand apart? One thing we often do is to make screenshots of competitive websites and analyze them. Later, we put our new design among them to see how it compares.

**5. Keep the page simple.**
The default is simplicity. Add graphic elements only for good reason, not to over-decorate.

**6. Simple navigation.**
Make the viewer take the fewest clicks possible to get where he or she is going. Also, make it easy for anyone to know where they are at any time when visiting your site—on what page and where in the hierarchy. An array of thumbnail images is a good way of stepping in and out of a collection.

**7. Make searchable on Google.**
Decide what on your site needs to be searchable, and put it in HTML words. Search engines like Google's can search only words, not pictures.

## 8. Get other people's opinions.
Use other people—friends, other photographers—to help give you an objective opinion and help you to stand back from what you are doing.

These are the key basic decisions, whether you are using an existing template or designing your own. Examples of templates (there are countless) are those supplied by processing software LightRoom, Apple's iWeb, and PhotoShelter. The examples I've chosen here and on the following pages, which of course are accessible online, all follow most of these commonsense principles. In each case, the photograph comes first, and it is no surprise that simplicity rules in all cases. What may be of interest is that one company specializing in website design and image storage recently surveyed online buyers of photography and found that more than 90 percent "hated" Flash-based introductions, and a similar proportion "hated" textured or graphical backgrounds. Decorate your website at your own risk!

**Michael Freeman (Top)**
*http://michaelfreemanphoto.com/*

**Sue Callister**
*http://www.suecallister.com/*

# BLACK & WHITE ON YOUR OWN SITE

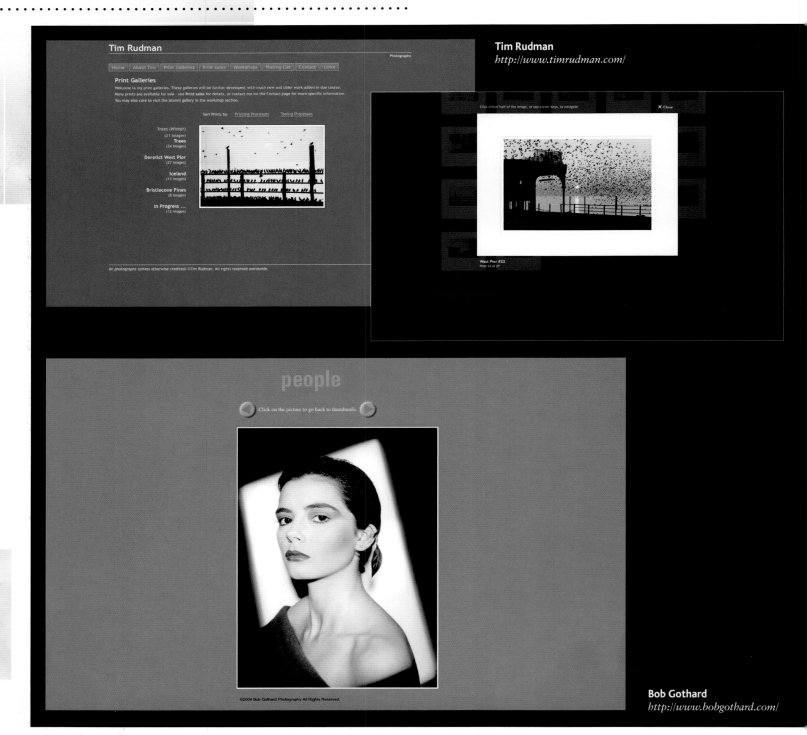

**Tim Rudman**
*http://www.timrudman.com/*

**Bob Gothard**
*http://www.bobgothard.com/*

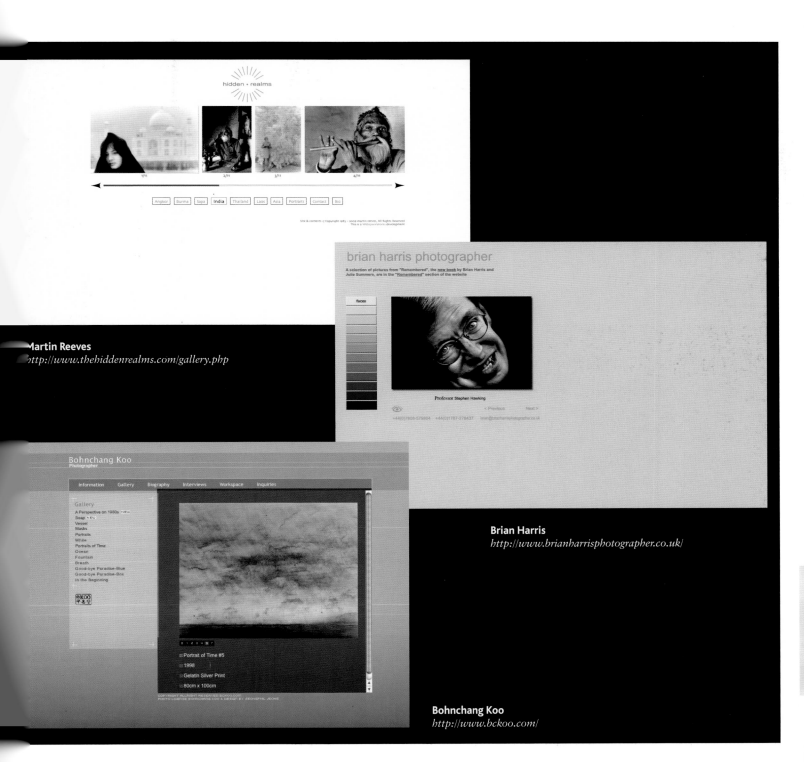

**Martin Reeves**
*http://www.thehiddenrealms.com/gallery.php*

**Brian Harris**
*http://www.brianharrisphotographer.co.uk/*

**Bohnchang Koo**
*http://www.bckoo.com/*

# GLOSSARY

**aperture** The opening behind the camera lens through which light passes on its way to the image sensor (CCD/CMOS).

**artifact** A flaw in a digital image.

**backlighting** The result of shooting with a light source, natural or artificial, behind the subject to create a silhouette or rim-lighting effect.

**ballast** The power pack unit for an HMI light which provides a high initial voltage.

**bit (binary digit)** The smallest data unit of binary computing, being a single 1 or 0.

**bit depth** The number of bits of color data for each pixel in a digital image. A photographic-quality image needs eight bits for each of the red, green, and blue channels, making for a bit depth of 24.

**boom** A support arm for attaching lights or fittings to.

**bracketing** A method of ensuring a correctly exposed photograph by taking three shots; one with the supposed correct exposure, one slightly underexposed, and one slightly overexposed.

**brightness** The level of light intensity. One of the three dimensions of color in the HSB color system. See also Hue and Saturation

**byte** Eight bits. The basic unit of desktop computing. 1,024 **bytes equals** one kilobyte (KB), 1,024 kilobytes equals one megabyte.

**CCD (Charge-Coupled Device)** A tiny photocell used to convert light into an electronic signal. Used in densely packed arrays, CCDs are the recording medium in most digital cameras.

**channel** Part of an image as stored in the computer; similar to a layer. Commonly, a color image will have a channel allocated to each primary color (e.g. RGB) and sometimes one or more for a mask or other effects.

**CMOS (Complementary Metal-Oxide Semiconductor)** An alternative sensor technology to the CCD, CMOS chips are used in ultra-high-resolution cameras from Canon and Kodak.

**CMYK (Cyan, Magenta, Yellow, Key)** The four process colors used for printing, including black (key).

**color gamut** The range of color that can be produced by an output device, such as a printer, a monitor, or a film recorder.

**color temperature** A way of describing the color differences in light, measured in Kelvins and using a scale that ranges from dull red (1900 K), through orange, to yellow, white, and blue (10,000 K).

**contrast** The range of tones across an image, from bright highlights to dark shadows.

**cropping** The process of removing unwanted areas of an image, leaving behind the most significant elements.

**depth of field** The distance in front of and behind the point of focus in a photograph, in which the scene remains in acceptable sharp focus.

**dialog box** An onscreen window, part of a program, for entering settings to complete a procedure.

**diffusion** The scattering of light by a material, resulting in a softening of the light and of any shadows cast. Diffusion occurs in nature through mist and cloud cover, and can also be simulated using diffusion sheets and soft-boxes.

**DMax (Maximum Density)** The maximum density—that is, the darkest tone—that can be recorded by a device.

**DMin (Minimum Density)** The minimum density—that is, the brightest tone—that can be recorded by a device.

**filter** (1) A thin sheet of transparent material placed over a camera lens or light source to modify the quality or color of the light passing through. (2) A feature in an image-editing application that alters or transforms selected pixels for some kind of visual effect.

**focal length** The distance between the optical center of a lens and its point of focus when the lens is focused on infinity.

**focal range** The range over which a camera or lens is able to focus on a subject (for example, 0.5m to Infinity).

**focus** The optical state where the light rays converge on the film or CCD to produce the sharpest possible image.

**fringe** In image-editing, an unwanted border effect to a selection, where the pixels combine some of the colors inside the selection and some from the background.

**frontal light** Light that hits the subject from behind the camera, creating bright, high-contrast images, but with flat shadows and less relief.

**f-stop** The calibration of the aperture size of a photographic lens.

**gamma** A measure of the contrast of an image, expressed as the steepness of the characteristic curve of an image.

**gobo** A corruption of "go between," this is anything used to block or partially block light.

**gradation** The smooth blending of one tone or color into another, or from transparent to colored in a tint. A graduated lens filter, for instance, might be dark on one side, fading to clear on the other.

**haze** The scattering of light by particles in the atmosphere, usually caused by fine dust, high humidity, or pollution. Haze makes a scene paler with distance, and softens the hard edges of sunlight.

**HDRI (High Dynamic Range Imaging)** A method of combining digital images taken at different exposures to draw detail from areas which would traditionally have been over or under exposed. This effect is typically achieved using a Photoshop plugin, and HDRI images can contain significantly more information than can be rendered on screen or even percieved by the human eye.

**histogram** A map of the distribution of tones in an image, arranged as a graph. The horizontal axis goes from the darkest tones to the lightest, while the vertical axis shows the number of pixels in that range.

**hot-shoe** An accessory fitting found on most digital and film SLR cameras and some high-end compact models, normally used to control an external flash unit. Depending on the model of camera, pass information to lighting attachments via the metal contacts of the shoe.

**HSB (Hue, Saturation, Brightness)** The three dimensions of color, and the standard color model used to adjust color in many image-editing applications.

**hue** The pure color defined by position on the color spectrum; what is generally meant by "color" in lay terms.

**ISO** An international standard rating for film speed, with the film getting faster as the rating increases. ISO 400 film is twice as fast as ISO 200, and will produce a correct exposure with less light and/or a shorter exposure. However, higher-speed film tends to produce more grain in the exposure, too.

**JPEG (Joint Photographic Experts Group)** Pronounced "jay-peg," a system for compressing images, developed as an industry standard by the International Standards Organization.

**layer** In image-editing, one level of an image file, separate from the rest, allowing different elements to be edited separately.

**LCD (Liquid Crystal Display)** Flat screen display used in digital cameras and some monitors. A liquid-crystal solution held between two clear polarizing sheets is subject to an electrical current, which alters the alignment of the crystals so that they either pass or block the light.

**light pipe** A clear plastic material that transmits like, like a prism or optical fiber.

**light tent** A tent-like structure, varying in size and material, used to diffuse light over a wider area for close-up shots.

**lumens** A measure of the light emitted by a lightsource, derived from candela.

**luminosity** The brightness of a color, independent of the hue or saturation.

**lux** A scale for measuring illumination, derived from lumens. It is defined as one lumen per square meter, or the amount of light falling from a light source of one candela one meter from the subject.

**mask** In image-editing, a grayscale template that hides part of an image. One of the most important tools in editing an image, it is used to limit changes to a particular area or protect part of an image from alteration.

**midtone** The parts of an image that are approximately average in tone, falling midway between the highlights and shadows.

**modelling light** A small light built into studio flash units which remains on continiously. It can be used to position the flash, approximating the light that will be cast by the flash.

**monobloc** An all-in-one flash unit with the controls and power supply built-in. Monoblocs can be synchronized together to create more elaborate lighting setups.

**noise** Random pattern of small spots on a digital image that are generally unwanted, caused by nonimage-forming electrical signals.

**open flash** The technique of leaving the shutter open and triggering the flash one or more times, perhaps from different positions in the scene.

**peripheral** An additional hardware device connected to and operated by the computer, such as a drive or printer.

**pixel (PICture ELement)** The smallest units of a digital image, pixels are the square screen dots that make up a bitmapped picture. Each pixel carries a specific tone and color.

**photoflood bulb** A special tungsten light, usually in a reflective dish, which produces an especially bright (and if suitably coated white) light. The bulbs have a limited lifetime.

**plug-in** In image-editing, software produced by a third party and intended to supplement a program's features or performance.

**power pack** The separate unit in flash lighting systems (other than monoblocks) which provides power to the lights.

**ppi (pixels-per-inch)** A measure of resolution for a bitmapped image.

**processor** A silicon chip containing millions of micro-switches, designed for performing specific functions in a computer or digital camera.

**Raw files** A digital image format, known sometimes as the "digital negative," which preserves higher levels of color depth than traditional 8 bits per channel images. The image can then be adjusted in software—potentially by three stops—without loss of quality. The file also stores camera data including meter readings, aperture settings and more. In fact each camera model creates its own kind of raw file, though leading models are supported by software like Adobe Photoshop.

**resolution** The level of detail in a digital image, measured in pixels (e.g. 1,024 by 768 pixels), or dots-per-inch (in a half-tone image, e.g. 1200 dpi).

**RGB (Red, Green, Blue)** The primary colors of the additive model, used in monitors and image-editing programs.

**saturation** The purity of a color, going from the lightest tint to the deepest, most saturated tone.

**scrim** a light open-weave fabric, used to cover softboxes.

**selection** In image-editing, a part of an on-screen image that is chosen and defined by a border in preparation for manipulation or movement.

**shutter speed** The time the shutter (or electronic switch) leaves the CCD or film open to light during an exposure.

**SLR (Single Lens Reflex)** A camera that transmits the same image via a mirror to the film and viewfinder, ensuring that you get exactly what you see in terms of focus and composition.

**TIFF (Tagged Image File Format)** A file format for bitmapped images. It supports CMYK, RGB and grayscale files with alpha channels, and lab, indexed-color, and it can use LZW lossless compression. It is now the most widely used standard for good-resolution digital photographic images.

**white balance** A digital camera control used to balance exposure and color settings for artificial lighting types.

# INDEX

# INDEX